Modularization

THE ART OF MAKING MORE
BY USING LESS

Modularization

ISBN: 978-91-87791-26-0
FIRST EDITION, FIRST PRINT
© RHEOLOGICA PUBLISHING, 2017

EDITOR: Karolina Modig

GRAPHIC DESIGN: Babak Shermond – theapartment.se

COVER: Babak Shermond

DISTRIBUTED BY: Rheologica Publishing – rheologica.com

PRINT: Bulls Graphics AB – Halmstad, 2017

To
Arvid
Vincent
& Leo

Modularization describes a new game plan for industries and businesses. It shows how leaders at companies and organizations need to think and what they need to do to be successful in the ever-increasing global arena.

In an easy-to-understand way, Martin describes what it takes to combine two competitive advantages, that are often difficult to reconcile, leading to double competitiveness. The book explains exactly how operations, through simple and smart means, can sharpen their competitive edge for the future. Though easy to read, the book is insightful and clever and can also be useful in graduate-level engineering or business and management programs.

PRESIDENT AND CEO, VOLVO GROUP

Martin Lundstedt

Acknowledgments

Many people have contributed in numerous ways to this book. First and foremost, I want to say a special thank-you to my amazing **family**, who have put up with my spending many hours behind closed doors and my introverted-writer temperament. Without their support, loyalty, and encouragement, this book would never have been written.

The **Jan Wallanders**, **Tom Hedelius**, and **Tore Browaldhs Foundation** have financed the research underlying this book, as well as several other academic publications. Without their support I would not have been able to carry out this research.

Martin Lundstedt, who during his time at *Scania* helped to initiate the study, has provided me with contacts and has been a wise and wonderful conversation partner. Thanks also to **Henrik Henriksson**, the current CEO of *Scania*, who in the same good spirit contributed many valuable comments and points of view.

I thank **everyone** who has allowed me to interview them and put up with my searching questions. It has been an absolute pleasure to attempt to fully appreciate what they do and then translate their knowledge and experiences into my own theories.

My colleagues at the Stockholm School of Economics, in particular **Niklas Modig**, have always been there for me to bounce ideas off them, making suggestions, seeing possibilities, and contributing endless amounts of energy. **Pär Åhlström** has read many earlier versions of the book, and his well-aimed and constructive criticism has helped me sharpen my thoughts and concepts. I also thank **Pär Mårtensson, Anders Richtnér, Mattias Axelson, Christer Karlsson, Åke Freij, Malin Schmidt, Erik Modig, Maria Booth, Lasse Lychnell,** and **Kerstin Wedin** for their encouragement, vital collegial support, and fellowhsip.

I have had a wonderful team behind the book: **Babak Shermond** from the design agency *The Apartment*, which with a master's hand has so uniquely and beautifully designed the layout of this book; **Karolina Modig**, for excellent proofreading and editing; **Charlotte Andersson** of the *Profile Agency*, for exemplary project leadership; and *Rheologica Publishing* and **Sheelagh Gaw**, for help with everything from sharing valuable experience to Lean publishing, distribution and translation.

Just when I though the book was ready to go to print, **Bengt Westerberg** unexpectedly contacted me, having read the manuscript in great detail, with many highly astute comments and well-directed questions. This was a hugely valuable help that led to a very important final polishing.

Finally, my warmest thanks go to **Kattis Ahlström**, whose contribution can be likened to that of a music teacher. Under her guidance I dared to try new notes and chords. She is also a remarkable person and has left an everlasting impression.

STOCKHOLM, MAY 2017

Martin Sköld

Table of contents

About the book

Modularization can be read in different ways: from cover to cover on a flight from *Stockholm* to *Paris*. By employees, managers, or the board of directors in an organization wanting to implement change and prepare themselves for the future; as a textbook within an operation, for the management team, or simply because you are curious to find out what you can learn from what the best do and how they think.

As this book is intended for all organizations, both small and large, the target group is also broad and includes everything from the public to the private sector and all types of industry including service operations, such as retail and healthcare, and knowledge-based operations, such as media.

THE POTENTIAL FOR DOUBLE COMPETITIVENESS

Let us start by exploring the potential to combine two advantages in a way that leads to **double competitiveness**. The first advantage, **cost-efficiency**, is achieved through efficient use of resources. This means that an operation can offer goods and services at low prices. The second advantage, **customization**, is about offering products or services tailored to individual customer needs. This means that goods and services can be offered at higher prices in the market. Combining these two advantages is a challenge as they operate in different ways and have different logics underlying them. However, doing so provides huge potential for those who succeed. We shall now see how they are connected and what lies behind the potential for **double competitiveness**.

CELL PHONE MESSAGE, 10 MARCH, 10:22

"Hi Martin, it's **Peter Paunovic!** I've been sitting here and thinking about your model and everything is becoming clearer and clearer, because of what it implies! I think you have created an $E=mc^2$ for businesses!

"What you describe, I see daily in the organizations I work with. Some of them are brilliant at providing customer benefits, and can tailor the goods and services they offer to match each customer's unique needs, but are hopeless when it comes to lowering costs. Other organizations are fantastic at keeping down costs. They do everything right, they are highly efficient, they follow procedures and standards to the letter, and they keep track of everything down to the very last detail, but they cannot adapt to meet individual customer needs. They have *zero* ability to customize!

"The model shows me where I need to direct my focus when helping companies. I can use this to explain, but also to explore ways forward. In discussions and in analyzing the needs of different businesses, I can use the model to illustrate how they can improve their performance. It's brilliant, Martin!"

WHY THIS BOOK WAS WRITTEN

Of course, Peter was over-exaggerating his enthusiasm for the model (after all he is himself a star media seller with many years of experience within the Metro Media sphere) and at that stage the model was far from fully developed. His call came around the time when I first realized that my own long-held view of what lay behind competitiveness had been somewhat narrow. Specifically, it was the day after a meeting at a hotel in Vaxholm, a small town in the Stockholm archipelago. We had been working with a management team and had long discussions about the structure and strategy for a newly started business. After many hours, our conversation began to center on how operations compete, in what way they were efficient, and how they create value and benefits. At that point, I showed them a model that I had been considering for a while and that distinguished between two types of competitiveness. But before I present the model here, let's first reflect on three separate experiences that illustrate different ways to compete and what they involve.

Skåne 1989

Throughout my childhood, my family ran a business that produced and sold parts for heavy trucks. My father was both owner and managing director, and the turnover was around 20 million dollars. I pretty much grew up there, in and around the warehouses and factory. By age 12 I could drive a forklift, and I drove a car before I was 15. Working there was very educational, and that was where I spent most of my free time on weekends and holidays.

Together with Jeff, a loyal and faithful employee, we were involved in setting up a business operation that made and sold shutters for fire trucks. These were really a kind of sliding door made from aluminum slats that could be opened quickly in tight spaces. Jeff was inventive and taught me how to think so that these shutters could be made as efficiently as possible. He devised new fixtures that helped us cut several aluminum slats at a time, and he came up with tools for applying the various seals quickly and easily. When one was working with Jeff, it was important to keep up. We did not take breaks until the work was completed. Jeff could not imagine interrupting work to take a break. I could see that my dad liked Jeff. He worked fast and efficiently and made more shutters than anyone else. He was the archetype of an efficient and hard worker. With his rapid pace and smart ways of working, we could make more shutters than the competition at significantly lower cost.

England 2011

Many years later I was in England visiting a very traditional factory that made exclusive and classic English furniture. I was given a guided tour of the factory by Angela, the company's sales manager. We followed the production flow and stopped at each machine. Angela was very knowledgeable and explained in a dedicated and pedagogical manner everything that went on in the factory. She knew the history of each machine and how each piece of equipment, purchased from all corners of the world, was perfectly suited to cope with the demanding and numerous manufacturing tasks.

Angela showed me the different types of wood they had imported from specialists across the US and Europe. She explained at great length how all the veneers were carefully selected and glued with precision onto core panels to create intricate patterns. Most of the employees had worked at the factory for many years and had unique knowledge about their area of expertise. During the tour I met an enthusiastic, older employee who explained that customers could always get the exact piece of furniture they wanted. "We do everything to meet the customer's unqiue requirements, so we never really make the same piece of furniture twice. But not everyone can afford to buy from us," he said, smiling proudly. "Our furniture is in a price class of its own, where customers are prepared and willing to pay for something unique."

Södertälje 2014

Three years after my visit to England, I was running a research project at Scania, a heavy truck manufacturer in Södertälje, Sweden. I interviewed the management team and met experts from development, production, sales, and marketing. All interviews provided a consistent picture: Scania's long tradition of sustainable and high profitability could be explained by its approach of creating close relationships with its customers, while at the same time using its resources in a very efficient way. Everyone I spoke with gave the same explanation — namely, that Scania and its customers work together hand in hand; if it goes well for the customers, then it will go well for Scania too. As a member of the marketing and sales team put it, "When we know what the customer really wants, then we can utilize our resources in the best way possible."

Another thing that struck me during my time at Scania was how familiar the management team was with details at all levels of the organization. They were aware of everything from engineering and technical matters to individual customer cases and demonstrated a remarkable ability to combine overall strategic vision with detailed insight and quick decision making. They switched effortlessly between engineering matters and customer or market issues, and customer dealings were always expressed in clear business parameters. What I saw at Scania was new and unlike anything I had ever seen before in any other operation.

COMPETITIVENESS AND VALUE

Growing up in and around my father's company and my visits to England and the furniture factory showed me that different types of operations often have very different ways of achieving competitiveness and creating value. Some operations create value through **cost-efficiency**, of which the business operated by Jeff at my father's company was a prime example. He paid great attention to detail and made the production of shutters highly efficient through his use of specially devised tools and fixtures to achieve high-volume production. Others create value through high **customization**, like the company in England with its customized furniture to fully meet each customer's unique requirements. But each of these approaches also has a problem. The problem with the shutters was that a limited number of models was available; a customer could not buy a tailored product. The problem with the furniture factory was that it was difficult to achieve a high level of cost-efficiency because tasks and materials were constantly being altered.

COST-EFFICIENCY provides advantages as low costs enable products and services to be put on the market at lower prices. Low costs are possible through an efficient use of resources, or how well an operation can use and employ its people, knowledge, processes, machines, equipment, and material.

CUSTOMIZATION provides advantages in the form of goods and services that are tailored to meet each individual customer's requirements. This allows the company to charge higher prices in the market because the customer is willing to pay for quality, features, functions, and performance that create special value and benefit.

What Peter Paunovic suddenly realized after our meeting in Vaxholm was that the operations and organizations he worked with were, at best, relying on only one out of two possible advantages. They were aiming for either cost-efficiency or customization, but not both. I call this phenomenon **single advantage**.

In the phone message that Peter left me, he went on to provide examples of operations that did everything right, where they followed standards and ensured that resources were fully utilized, and other operations that adapted their ways of working and the products they offered to suit the customer. With the help of the model, Peter could see the same pattern I had seen: most operations and organizations create value through optimizing *either* cost-efficiency *or* customization.

THE POTENTIAL FOR DOUBLE COMPETITIVENESS

In my role at the Stockholm School of Economics, studying and explaining competitiveness forms an important part of my teaching and research. Over the years, I have worked with many different businesses and organizations in various research projects, as a teacher or in improvement efforts. I have met many managers and employees whose ambition has been to make their operations as good as they can possibly be through aligning themselves with one distinct competitive advantage. Make a choice and stick to it, you could say. Consider the situation in your operation and talk with your boss about it. Or read a newspaper and see what is happening in other businesss. What is being said about competitiveness? What type of value is being created? How do we think that we create value?

When I started to work more closely with Scania, I realized that it was possible to combine the two competitive advantages of cost-efficiency and customization to create a smart, profitable, and coherent whole, thus releasing **a potential for double advantage.** This was the insight that led to the obvious delight in Peter's message. By seeing that both were attainable, Peter had now realized what I had seen for myself at Scania: a way to offer new advice and guidance when assisting various organizations and management teams.

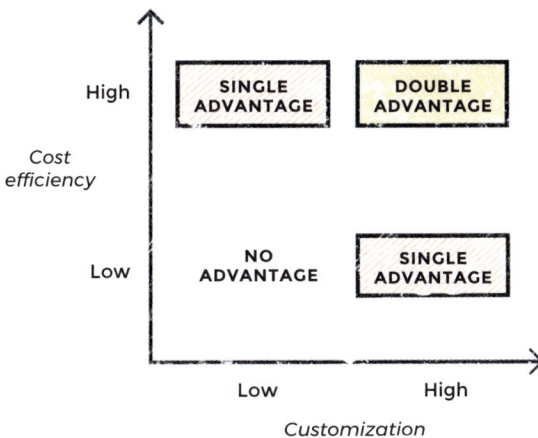

Cost efficiency

	Low	High
High	SINGLE ADVANTAGE	DOUBLE ADVANTAGE
Low	NO ADVANTAGE	SINGLE ADVANTAGE

Customization

Releasing a potential for **double advantage** enables companies and organizations to benefit from **double competitiveness**. Cost-efficiency is about employees doing the right thing every day, where machines will be running at capacity, and where materials, information, and knowledge will be used in ways that lead to high resource utilization at all times. Customization is about goods and services being adapted to match each customer's unique requirements in terms of quality, performance, and characteristics in a way that the customer really values.

This book is about **how to release** the often-overlooked potential that enables double competitiveness. It is easier than you think. It is there, it is just not being used. I am convinced that all operations can succeed in this way — both large and small ones, whether an industrial company, a service company, a school, within healthcare, a bank, the finance sector, insurance, media, or the public sector.

We will look at examples from different branches and companies. Scania will be our prime example, but we will also see what we can learn from a chef, a stylist, and the world's largest toy manufacturer, Lego. You will be given tools and models that will explain, step by step, how you can succeed in this undertaking.

SUMMARY
–CHAPTER–
ONE

In this chapter, we have identified a potential that can be created when operations combine two types of competitiveness.

→ Cost-efficiency, which enables lower costs through the efficient utilization of resources.

→ Customization, which enables higher revenues through offering products and services which are adapted to meet customer requirements.

→ Many operations rely on single competitiveness, which means that either cost-efficiency or customization dominates.

→ By aiming for double competitiveness, a potential is released to combine the advantages of both cost-efficiency and customization.

In the next chapter, we shall explore the mechanisms that lie behind cost-efficiency and customization to better understand why most operations tend to rely on only one of these two competitive advantages.

CHAPTER TWO

VOLUME OR VARIETY?

In this chapter we will look more closely at why so many operations rely on single competitivness and see that it is because two forces are pulling in opposite directions. One is pulling towards creating value through producing **high volume**, where goods and services are **general**. The other force is pulling towards **wide variety** where goods and services are **specific** and customized to meet each customer's unique needs. These two strong driving forces are acting in opposite directions and are difficult to manage and change.

WHY DO OPERATIONS RELY ON
SINGLE COMPETITIVENESS?

Let's meet Sven, who is thinking about changing his job. He has an interview and is faced with two options on how to get there. Considering Sven's situation through both a customer and an operational perspective can help us to understand why companies and operations limit themselves to single competitiveness. What can we see when we look at both of these perspectives?

Sven is thinking about changing jobs

Sven works for the finance department at his local government offices. For the last few years, he has been considering whether it is time for a change. Purely by chance he sees a job advertisement: a small plumbing business is looking for a financial director. He submits his CV. After a few weeks, the managing director of the plumbing company contacts Sven and asks if they can meet. Just the thought that he might be one step closer to making a life-changing decision makes Sven feel unwell. The meeting is to be at 8:30 a.m. at the plumbing company offices, but Sven decides to take the whole day off work.

While Sven irons his new white shirt, he ponders about the best way to get to the plumbing company. Usually he walks or bicycles to work; occasionally, if he has a longer journey due to a meeting, he takes the subway. In this instance, he is unsure of how long the journey will take and does not like the idea of having to jostle for space with other commuters. To be on the safe side, he decides to leave the apartment two hours before the interview. "But is it really worth getting up so early?" he wonders as he hangs up his freshly ironed shirt.

Of course getting a cab would be an alternative, but Sven rarely takes a cab and is unsure of how much it would cost. Anyway, he doesn't feel it is right for him to indulge in such a luxury. The advantage, of course, would be that he would not get sweaty on the way to the station or have to worry about finding his way from the subway station to the office at the other end. Sven also thinks it would be nice, just once, not to fight with the crowds on the subway and all those people with colds. He guesses that a cab would not cost more than $50. He compares this price to the cost of a standard subway ticket, which is $3.

SUBWAY OR CAB?

Sven's deliberations reveal that he has to decide between two alternatives, which provide quite different solutions to his needs. But what is he actually thinking about? What features characterize operations like the subway and the cab company?

Affordable or exclusive?

We know that Sven has extensive subway experience. Maybe that is why he cannot decide. On the one hand, he sees the subway as good value for his money with the standard $3 ticket price. On the other hand, he thinks that the journey will be complicated, physically demanding, and time-consuming. He will need to spend time and energy walking to the station, change subway lines, and then figure out how to get from the subway station to the plumbing company's offices. Taking the subway will help him with part of his needs; he will be transported part of the way, but not all the way.

We also get the impression that Sven does not have as much experience of cabs. He does not know what it will cost, he guesses around $50, quite a bit more than the $3 for a standard subway ticket. Of course the cab costs more, but there is value in it. He believes that a cab will be quicker than the subway. It will be more comfortable and a more flexible and easier alternative, as he will be picked up at his home and transported door to door. Taking a cab is therefore a more exclusive option, which comes at a higher price.

Seeing it from Sven's viewpoint, and therefore taking the customer's view, we can see that the subway and a cab offer different types of value. The subway is an example of an operation that provides **affordable** options, but which cannot be customized to suit an individual customer's needs. Simply put, it offers the same thing to everyone. In the same way, the cab company is a good example of an operation that provides **exclusive** options designed to address each individual customer's needs and requirements in a unique way, but which comes at a higher price.

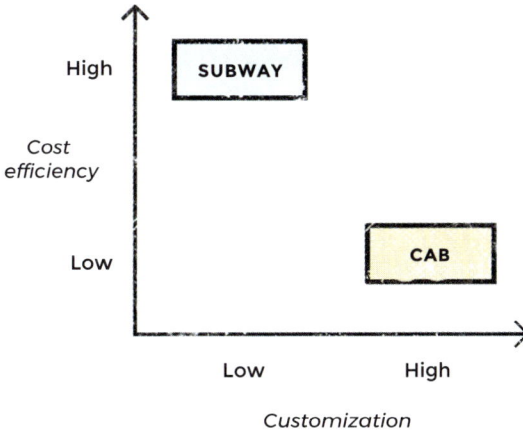

When we compare the cab option with the subway option, we can see that they are two extremes at opposite ends of a diagonal line that differentiates between price and level of customization.

Volume or variety?

Seeing it from an operational perspective, Stockholm's subway system has been in action since 1933, when it started with one tunnel under the Södermalm district of Stockholm. It has gradually expanded in different phases, most recently in 1994. The entire tunnel system is just over 100 km long and is a result of huge investments in earthworks, tunnels, track, stations, trains, and coaches. No one really knows what the exact cost to build it has been, but according to Svevia, which builds, operates, and maintain Sweden's roads and infrastructure, a good estimate at today's prices would be around 1 billion Swedish kronor (or about $0.1 billion U.S.) per kilometer. In other words, it would cost $10 billion to build the entire subway system today. This is comparable with other subways in other cities and countries around the world. To make such a huge investment economically viable, one must generate high volumes. In this case, at least 700,000 passengers per day need to use the system so that the costs can be divided across a sufficient number of people. Therefore, **high volume** is the reason for the low ticket price.

To start a cab firm requires a relatively low investment. Cars can be used on existing roads, and a cab booking system can be purchased and set up relatively cheaply. An entrepreneur can quickly get started with a small financial investment. But the cab has a very different business model from the subway system. Each cab passenger wants to go to a specific address, and therefore the cab often carries just one passenger at a time. For this reason, volume is low. At the same time, the cab offers wider variety: it picks up people from an unlimited number of different addresses and drops them off at other addresses. This makes cabs a more exclusive alternative. To compensate for this low volume and **wide variety**, the cab will need to charge a significantly higher price per trip than the subway.

From the operations perspective, the subway and the cab have different conditions. For the subway, **high volume** is essential if the prices are to be kept low. For the cab, high prices are needed to compensate for the low volume and **wide variety**. We can thus see that we look at things in different ways depending on whether we are looking at it from the customer's or the operation's perspective.

THE REASON FOR SINGLE COMPETITIVENESS

We can find plenty more examples in other branches. Banks, financial companies, and insurance companies are similar to the subway, in that they offer general products that can be offered to large customer groups: for example, savings accounts, index funds, mortgages, and home insurance policies. Schools are another example of standardization, as students follow a predetermined teaching plan and schedules are drawn up in advance. Operations in the building industry, furniture, and interior design are a third example, since materials and fixtures and fittings are sold in standardized dimensions and sizes.

There are also many examples where, like the cab, offers are exclusive and specific. A house may be uniquely designed by an architect to meet a specific customer's needs. Tailors make clothes according to a specific person's measurements for ultimate fit and comfort. Even in the consulting branch, more and more customized solutions are being offered within finance, law, strategic planning, and management to match specific customer needs.

Customers can thus choose between two completely different types of offers: goods and services that are **general and affordable** or **exclusive and specific**. This is because companies that offer these solutions need either to create **high volume** or to manage **wide variety** in order to be productive and profitable. Double advantage is not a selectable option.

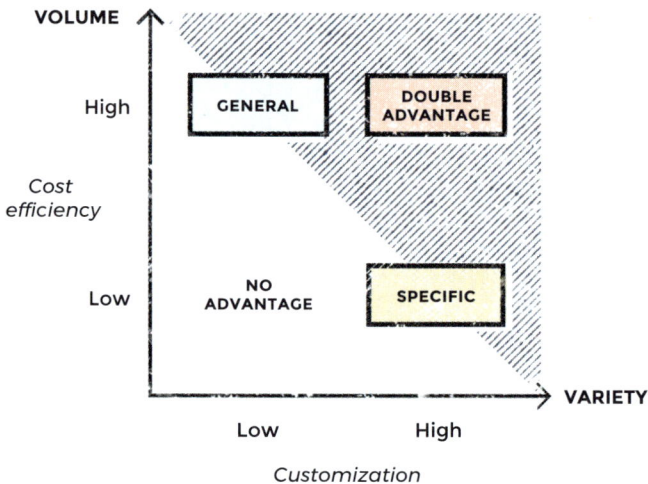

But do you think Sven is happy with the two alternatives he is faced with?

If we look at the characteristics of subway travel versus cab travel and apply them to our model, we can see two things. First, companies that resemble the subway will find themselves in the top left-hand corner of the model, in the form of general offers produced from high volume operations. Second, operations reminiscent of the cab will be found at the bottom right-hand corner of the model, where there are exclusive and specific offers from wide variety.

This explains why many companies and organizations find it difficult to achieve double competitiveness. They are fully occupied with activities that either optimize high volume, or wide variety. The challenge that operations face is that the model is divided in two along a diagonal line and creates two halves. The grey area does not exist — at least, not for companies that share similarities with subways or cab companys. This means that competitiveness is achieved through two strong forces pulling in opposite directions. One force tries to optimize efficiency from high volume, whilst the other tries to optimize effectiveness from wide variety.

This leads to a **dilemma**. Companies and organizations that offer general products find it difficult to deal with demands for variety. However, those that offer a wide variety of products find it difficult to benefit from the advantages of producing high volumes. Double competitiveness is simply not an option or viable alternative. In a competitive situation, the response is as follows: operations that compete on high volume try to find new ways to increase volume even more, and those that compete by offering wide variety try to further increase the variety they offer. But these two strategies reinforce the dilemma, making it even more difficult to achieve double competitiveness. Many companies and organizations are therefore trapped in behaviors that are difficult to escape from and change. Higher volumes or even greater variety can be perceived as rational and the right strategy, but these actions serve only to reinforce a single competitiveness even more.

SUBWAY DOOR-TO-DOOR

We have good grounds to assume that Sven is not representative of a typical future customer. In the near future, our world will be full of people who have grown up with totally different perspectives and habits and who have grown accustomed to the wide range of services that services like Spotify, Airbnb, AirDine, Uber, and the like offer. The younger generation will demand more customization and more convenient options. People will think about value and about taking responsibility — value for themselves and responsibility for issues related to the use of natural resources and the environment.

Double competitiveness is a way to think long-term in order to survive and meet the future. To do this, we need to find a way to control the mechanisms that drive volume and variety in opposite directions, leading operations to be either efficient or effective but not both.

SUMMARY
– CHAPTER –
TWO

In this chapter we have investigated the mechanisms that lie behind operations relying on single competitiveness.

→ We have seen that single competitiveness occurs because two strong forces are pulling in opposite directions, towards either;

↳ high volume which leads to the supply of general products and services, or

↳ wide variety, which leads to the supply of products and services which are specific and customized.

→ Volume and variety are two strong driving forces that steer what operations do and what they offer their customers.

→ Combining high volume and wide variety is difficult to achieve because the integrated mechanisms to achieve both goals are missing. Therefore, subways work one way and cabs in another. This explains the single competitiveness phenomena.

In the next chapter, we will find out what we can learn from a company that for many decades has demonstrated double competitiveness. A company that for a long time has beaten the trade-off between volume and variety.

CHAPTER THREE

THE BLACK SWAN

We will now look at a company that since 1947 has managed to release the potential that allows for **double competitiveness**. This has been achieved by following an established method and some clear principles. This chapter aims to describe what this company has done and what lies behind their success in achieving the combination of high volume and wide variety.

THE TOUGHEST INDUSTRY
SECTOR IN THE WORLD

The automotive industry is often described as the most competitive industry sector in the world. There are several reasons for this. It has a long history, which means that many companies are competing in this space and offering similar products. Also, large cyclical swings can occur in a short time, and the market can rise or fall by as much as 30% to 50% in one year. A third reason is the high levels of overcapacity, almost 30%, that occur because the companies have no built-in flexibility in their production. Fourth, the sector has unusually high cost pressures. Costs are driven by ever-changing regulatory requirements, the need to introduce new technology, and because competition is intense new products need to be launched into the market quickly.

All these factors add up to the fact that companies in this industry sector are subject to extremely high costs, which they need to cover. One way to address these costs is to continually introduce improvements and increase efficiency. It is generally acknowledged that efficiency, usually in the form of cost savings, must be increased by 5% each year for a business to maintain its profitability or competitiveness. Therefore, new strategies and methods are continually being devised and introduced to develop and produce in new and ever more efficient ways. The harsh environment within the industry has forced companies to continually re-evaluate and be prepared to change even well-established methods.

Another way to deal with these high costs is through economies of scale, which can be achieved through producing high volumes. High volumes enable costs to be spread out over as large a number of products as possible. The quest for economies of scale explains why we have seen so many mergers and acquisitions in recent years. We are lured into thinking that they will provide the best conditions for meeting our competition. It is widely perceived that high volume is the be-all and end-all when it comes to success.

THE BLACK SWAN

But in the automotive industry, there is a black swan. A relatively small company, **Scania** from Södertälje, Sweden can be seen as a contradiction to the widespread assumption that high volume is the most vital necessity for survival in the industry. Scania is barely a third of the size of some of its main competitors, but has still managed the feat of maintaining an unbroken profitability record over the last 60 years. Moreover, Scania generate a profit twice that of its competitors.

With its relatively small size, in terms of the number of vehicles it sells per year, Scania does not align with the prevailing theories of economies of scale and competitive advantages. According to these theories, Scania should not be able to achieve such high profitability because its production volume is simply too small. Even more difficult to understand is how Scania manages to be profitable while tailoring and customizing its products so extensively. Such customizing should lead to even higher costs and lower profitability.

Are the theories wrong, or have we missed something that Scania has discovered? What is the secret? What does Scania do that others do not?

THE CUSTOMER IS AT
THE CENTER

Scania explains its profitability in terms of always putting the customer first. This can be seen in several ways. One way is that Scania's business model focuses on improving all customers' profitability. Through its knowledge of the customers' operations and actual needs, Scania can provide solutions that improve the customer's profitability. Scania's business model takes into account customers' revenue potential and total operating costs. The customer is the focus of Scania's value chain.[1]

Interest in customers also permeates Scania's leadership. Leif Östling, who was Scania's CEO for 18 years, used to say that the company culture should mirror the customer base, or otherwise the distance to the customer would be too great. Another example I heard was about Scania's former CEO, Martin Lundstedt. During a dinner with an international customer, he could provide an account of the customer's history with Scania over the last 40 years, what trucks the customer had bought, and in what order various events had taken place. The current CEO, Henrik Henriksson, often speaks in great detail about the factors that underlie a customer's profitability and what solutions Scania can provide to help customers be profitable. Within Scania, it is said that profitable customers are the ultimate proof of customer value. A profitable customer is also a satisfied customer.

Scania's interest in and closeness to its customers are very apparent in the business's operations. Employees talk about customers and customer value in a way that is rarely heard of. They seem better able to express customers' needs then the customers themselves, in terms of business imperatives, engineering, and the factors that influence revenue and drive costs. Engineering and business issues are very closely connected.

THE CRISIS

Scania has not always been a success story. After the Second World War, Scania was a damaged company with a bad reputation and poor-quality products. The company had pushed forward with a new range of products that later proved to be of low quality. The materials used in the new products had been insufficiently tested prior to use. Furthermore, resources were in short supply and European suppliers could not meet demand. Important parts could not be sourced, or if they could, they were of substandard quality. As a result, the entire new product range lacked quality. Customers lost faith in the company and it was generally accepted that Scania was in crisis.[2]

Sverker Sjöström was recruited in 1947 to rescue Scania from these problems. He had a background in engineering physics from the Royal Institute of Technology in Stockholm and a licentiate degree from the Solid Mechanics Department. Sjöström, then only 27 years old, quickly noted that Scania had computed forces and wear in a way that did not provide an accurate picture of the stresses to which materials were actually subjected. His research background and experience in computational methods, with high demands for theoretical analysis and experimental testing, provided the basis for the method he decided to employ to solve the problem.[1,2]

MODULARIZATION

During Sjöström's first year at Scania, the seeds were sown for the method which would become known as "**modularization**." This would be the basis for the company's future development strategy: with a limited number of components, produce an almost unlimited number of truck variations to offer each customer the optimal solution for his or her needs.[3] The goal was to customize solutions for each customer's unique requirements. Modularization is therefore about creating a vast number of possible combinations with as few components as possible. Becoming better at adapting trucks to meet customer needs would mean better profitability for the customer.[4] Everything starts and finishes with the customer, Scania maintained.[5]

The work with modularization follows a structure in which the truck is divided into different engineering areas: engines, chassis, frames, cabs, hubs, and axles. Each area has its own set of components, such as the set of components needed to build a complete engine. These different technological areas, called **component groups**, also reflect how Scania is organized.

In turn, each **component group** contains a large number of parts needed to build a complete engine, a chassis, or a frame. These parts are sorted within a structure where Scania differentiates between **component series** and **performance steps**. These in turn describe which parts are needed and the variations required to meet the demands of specific customers and customer groups. These parts form the "modules" and can be combined with each other in lots of different ways. The number of performance steps within a component series is carefully worked out and considered in relation to the demands of different customer groups. The goal is for each part, or component, to be of optimal design in terms of strength, weight, and quality.[4]

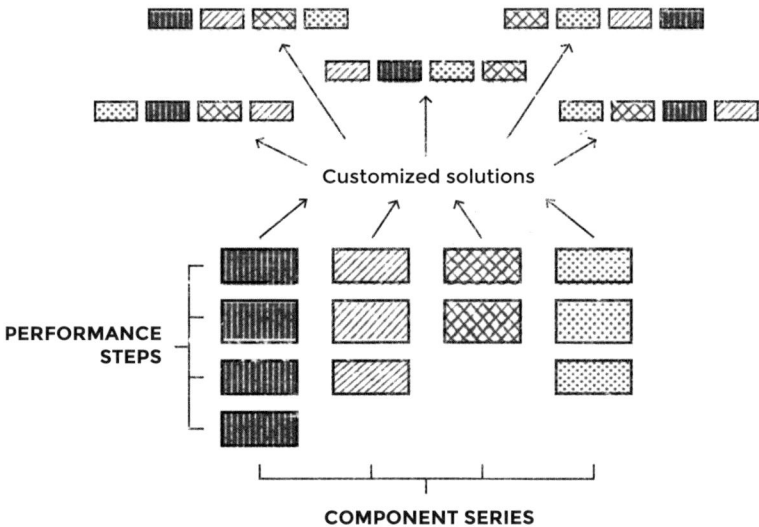

Customized solutions

PERFORMANCE STEPS

COMPONENT SERIES

The number of performance steps is therefore subject to a trade-off. On one hand, there must be a sufficient number of them to meet the customer's changing demands for customized solutions. On the other hand, there should not be too many, because the development and production costs would be too high and the volume too low. Performance steps are therefore very important in explaining why Scania uses significantly fewer components than its competitors.

Sverker Sjöström explains this consideration in the following way: "Before a component can be considered really good from both a functional and a cost perspective, it requires years of hard work. By the time the component nears its optimal state, large costs have been incurred in order for the component to be able to do what it is supposed to do at the lowest production cost possible in relation to the quality level that has been decided on. It is therefore important that the costs should be split across as many components as possible. This means that we have to keep the number of components to a minimum in order to achieve the highest volumes possible. That is, we need to share as many components and details across all our vehicles as possible and, as far as possible, avoid special models. A component must be used for as long as possible. Then we have sufficient time to ensure that it is optimally designed, produced rationally, and burdened by only a very small amount of the total development costs."[2]

To combine the different components and enable tailored customer solutions, they first need to fit together. This is possible through something called standardized **interfaces**. Interfaces can be compared to "pairing points" and describe how one component matches and can connect with another component. Interfaces can look very different. For example, they can be represented by a surface between two components, or they can describe an area or give information about how one part fits together with another part. Interfaces are the basis on which parts can be fitted together and combined.

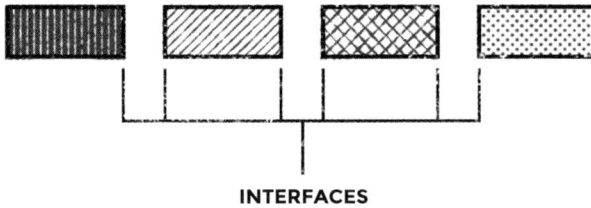

INTERFACES

Scania has chosen to use the same interfaces for a long time, and this strategy has definite advantages. For example, it allows for the individual parts to be developed separately. It also enables the very important capability of being able to remove and exchange parts without affecting surrounding parts. In this way, Scania can develop specific parts, such as engines, without affecting other parts such as gearboxes or cabs. This simplifies work and forms the basis for continual improvement. A new Scania truck is always better than an earlier version. With the help of interfaces, Scania can work with continuous improvement in small stages that are simple and can be reliably introduced into the process.[4,5]

Scania's use of the modularization method, consisting of some clearly defined principles, explains why they have succeeded in achieving wide variety and been able to customize customer solutions, whilst at the same time achieving high volume.

Let us summarize the method of modularization and the principles.

MODULARIZATION is a way of thinking that provides a huge scope for creating customized products and reaching high volume in parts produced.

COMPONENT GROUPS represent a way of sorting the products offered into smaller categories of parts, which have similarities and belong together. An operation can also be organized around its component groups.

A COMPONENT SERIES is a lower classification of parts within a component group.

PERFORMANCE STEPS are the variations of a component within a component series that allow for variety within the products available.

INTERFACES are the information or knowledge that expresses how components fit together and can be combined.

MODULES are the collective name for all components or parts that are found in a component series and performance steps and can be combined with each other.

HAS MODULARIZATION PROVED
PROFITABLE FOR SCANIA?

Employees from Scania are often asked if modularization has proved profitable. The answer is that for Scania, modularization is so complex that it can be measured only by its results. By that I mean that a 60-year period of unbroken profitability speaks for itself. According to Scania's own calculations, if the number of components were reduced by half, costs would be cut by 30% to 50% within research and development, 10% in production, and roughly 30% in sales and services.[5]

WHAT DOES SCANIA DO?

We have now familiarized ourselves with Scania and seen how this relatively small company challenges its competitors. Partly due to its unusually long and profitable history and partly through its remarkable ability to combine customized products with high volume production. Scania manage to challenge established theories on economies of scale despite having significantly lower total production volumes than its competitors, and at the same time offer a much higher level of customized products.

What is it that Scania do?

We have seen that Scania use a method called modularization. With the help of this method **Scania manage to combine two types of competitiveness** which provides them with a **double advantage**. Modularization is therefore a method which eliminates the need to make the trade-off we saw in chapter 2, between volume and variety. It enables resources to be used very efficiently whilst at the same time allows goods and services to be adapted and tailored to meet each customer's unique needs.

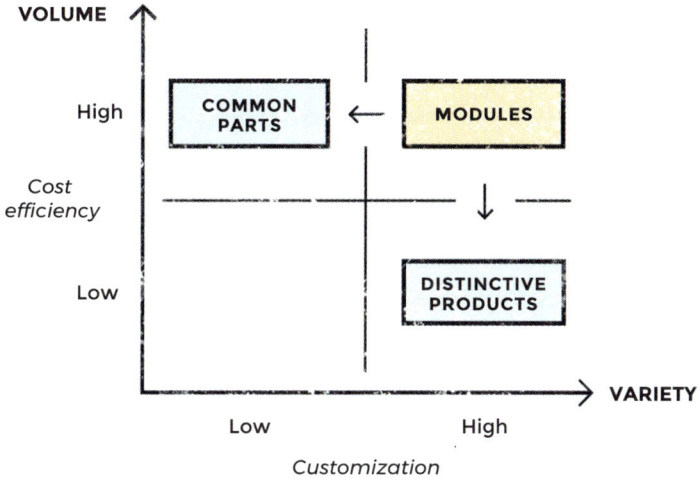

At the core of modularization lie the modules. Modules are parts of an offer which can be combined with other parts, and when these are combined in many different ways they create distinctive and customized products. This is how modularization generates wide variety, and the high volume is achieved when the same module is used in many different final products. Modularization and modules are what lie behind both being able to customize goods and services, and achieving high volume in terms of common parts.

CHAPTER THREE

SUMMARY
— CHAPTER —
THREE

In this chapter we have found out how Scania achieve double competitiveness.

→ Scania puts the customer first by providing customized solutions, which means offering wide variety.

→ Scania manages to produce high volumes, which allows for the efficient use of resources.

→ This combination is achieved through a method Scania call modularization, where modules are the units that enable the conditions for both volume and variety.

To learn more thoroughly from Scania, the next two chapters will look more closely at the factors that lie behind Scania's success. In the next chapter, we will look at what enables Scania to achieve effective variety. In chapter 5, we will look at what lies behind Scania's ability to achieve efficient volume.

CHAPTER FOUR

VARIETY

Let us take a closer look at the concept of variety to really understand **what it takes to maximize effectiveness in terms of variety**. Using some examples to help us, we will see that different operations have different potential for offering variety. We will then, with the help of modules, try to understand how to achieve effectiveness in terms of the variety we can provide.

HEDBERGS

A few miles from where I grew up was a well-established furniture shop. Visiting it was like stepping back into another,
more elegant world. Even my siblings and I, generally pretty wild, were struck by the atmosphere inside and always
behaved a little bit better. Considering that the shop was in
the middle of the countryside and fairly remote, it had an
uncommonly wide and exclusive selection. Because of word-
of-mouth reports on the excellent service and the extensive
and luxurious section of items it offered, customers traveled
from far and wide to visit the shop. It was run by a true entrepreneur and was open every day of the week. However,
despite all this, today Hedberg's is just a distant memory.

It isn't that Hedberg's had a particularly challenging starting position. Of course, running an exclusive furniture shop
in such a rural location is difficult, but Hedberg's became
something of an attraction. Neither the owner's ambition nor
the distance from customers stood in the way of the company's ambitions. Rather, the reason for Hedberg's eventual
decline was it had taken on a task that was too difficult. The
extensive selection of goods it offered was bought in small
volumes from many different suppliers and manufacturers. A
lot of time was spent in administration and investing in these
numerous relationships. A wide variety in small volumes,
with expensive shipments and high storage costs, gradually
ate away at margins and profitability.

Hedberg's is an example of a type of company that is quite common. They typically buy items for resale to customers: one sofa in, one sofa out, etc. This type of company can only increase the variety it offers by purchasing more and varied items, for example the same sofa in different colors, or sofas of different designs. This is how they respond to customers with different demands.

However, the more items they purchase, the larger the levels of stock they hold, which increases administration costs and ties up capital. They may be able to offer a wide selection of products, but this type of company has a limited ability to influence its **effectiveness in variety**, because what goes in is always the same as what goes out; a sofa in is still a sofa out.

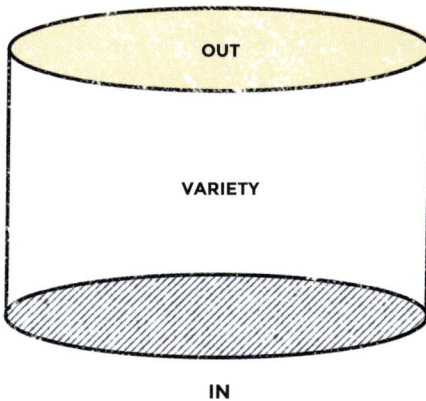

It would be fair to say that Hedberg's became a victim of low effectiveness in variety, which ate away at its profitability. At the same time, we know that many other businesses operate in this way, particularly in the retail branch. What do they do to avoid this problem?

First, we can see that the retail sector is now dominated by larger stores and chains. The larger you are, the more able you are to negotiate your purchase prices and, in this way, squeeze your margins to your own advantage. Another way to be more effective is to get to know your customers so well that you know exactly what they want. This avoids unnecessary variety in the goods you stock, goods that do not add customer value and only tie up capital unnecessarily. It is also common to buy goods on consignment, meaning that someone else, usually a supplier, pays for you to promote their goods in your store. Another way is to buy in goods against a customer order — for example, if a customer wants a sofa in a different color from the sofa you have in the store. A fifth way is to work with a supplier who has a wide and varied selection, instead of buying from several different suppliers. This keeps administrative costs down. Even increasing prices can be an alternative, but this is difficult as customers are usually well informed about the prices of competitors.

REFRIGERATORS AND CLOSETS

I am sure that, like me, you have often looked into your refrigerator and ascertained that there is nothing in it from which you can make a meal, even though the refrigerator is far from empty. Or you looked in your closet, full of clothes, and found nothing to wear. It is as if they are both full and empty at the same time. Why is that? Let us look at a chef and stylist, to see how they tackle these problems.

Nutritious and healthy food

Alexandra Zazzi[1] is a chef who has owned restaurants, written cookbooks, and participated in numerous radio and television shows. She often talks about how we need to live a healthier and more wholesome life, and that the key is to take control over what we eat. Cooking nutritious and healthy meals, according to Alexandra, should not take a lot of extra time.

In an article that I read recently, Alexandra presented a list of ingredients that she described as essential to keep at home. The list was divided into five categories, which she termed base items. Alexandra believes that these **base items** form the foundation for preparing nutritious and varied meals with as few ingredients as possible.

Having reflected a little on Alexandra's way of thinking and working, I made a simple calculation. With 33 ingredients, I could quickly come up with over 40 recipes for completely different meals. In addition, if you use this list as your grocery list, buying food is quicker and will enable you to keep a good check on price differences. It is not just a way to create meals; it also has advantages in the form of saving time and money.

CHAPTER FOUR

Improving your style

In a totally separate context, I happened to read about stylist Jenny Ragnwald.[2] She has always been interested in clothes and fashion. Jenny has worked with fashion brand names such as InWear, Zadig & Voltaire, Mulberry, and Maria Westerlind, and she has worked at the exclusive department store NK in Stockholm. Today Jenny works as a personal shopper and stylist. She helps her customers with style advice by suggesting a more varied wardrobe, with clothes that can be used for a wide variety of occasions.

To create a wardrobe that is versatile and allows for clothes to be mixed and matched in many different ways, Jenny has what she calls wardrobe **base items**. The idea is to divide the items in your wardrobe into different types that can be combined with each other to create different outfits. In this way, you create a large number of wardrobe combinations without needing masses of different items. As a rough estimate, I have 14 items in my closet that can generate 26 different outfits.

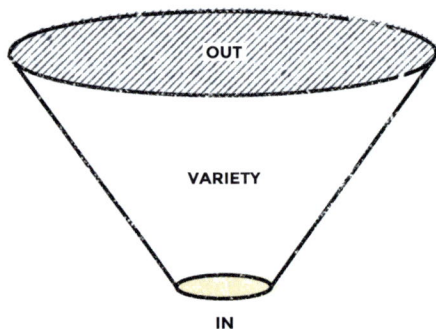

Thinking like Alexandra and Jenny has many advantages. You could say that it is about getting more out than you put in, in terms of meals and outfits, from ingredients or items of clothing. This demonstrates a way of thinking that allows for **high effectiveness in variety.**

What you experience when you look into your refrigerator and see that it is full but that nothing can be put together to make a decent meal is low effectiveness in variety. It is the same when you observe that your closet is full of clothes but you have nothing to wear. This is because the food you have or the clothes hanging in your closet were all bought at different times. They are all different, but nothing goes together because they are difficult to combine. We have bought food or clothes that we cannot use. That is why we think the refrigerator or closet is full yet empty at the same time.

CREATIVE AND OPEN-ENDED PLAY

The examples of basic food and wardrobe items presented above illustrate something that provides customers with clear advantages. Let us now consider the world's largest toy manufacturer, Lego, which truly knows how to succeed in business through effectiveness in variety. For decades Lego has captivated children, teenagers, and adults alike with its creative and open-ended play. By combining the small interlocking, plastic bricks in different ways and packaging them in different sets, Lego has achieved impressive and seemingly infinite variety. This is an important explanation as to how Lego has succeeded in becoming the biggest in the world when it comes to making toys.

"Leg godt"

Lego derives its name from the Danish phrase *leg godt*, which translates to "play well." That is what the company's goal has always been: to stimulate creativity and development through play and learning, where anyone can always build something good in only a short time. Lego bricks were first created in 1949 by Godtfred Kirk Christiansen, based on the Kiddicraft Self-locking Bricks.[5] They were produced under the name Lego Basic, a name that defined what the Lego pieces looked like: bricks with single or double rows of studs on the top, which can be attached onto or under another brick with studs.

Over the years Lego has undertaken many collaborations, notably with the film industry. In 1999, Darth Vader and Lego Star Wars appeared. Harry Potter followed a few years later, and after that the successful Lego Movie was released, which earned $469 million worldwide. The demand for Lego is enormous. Not only children play with Lego, but adults do too. In the USA they are known as AFOLs, short for Adult Fans of Lego, and there are online chat rooms especially designed for adult Lego builders. There are many professional

Lego sculptors who earn their living by creating replicas of buildings around the world.[6]

Most Lego pieces are sold in sets. Since 1955 Lego has released 4,270 different sets aimed at different age groups, to attract as many different target groups as possible. For the younger children, there is Duplo, with 53 different sets available including trucks, tractors, farms, space rockets and animals. There is also Lego Technic, aimed at an older and more discerning age group. And there are some very advanced and expensive sets made up of thousands of pieces; among these you can find the world famous Taj Mahal, which can be built using a staggering 5,922 Lego pieces.[6] Lego has calculated that six bricks, with two rows of four studs, can be combined in a total of 915,103,765 different ways.

Lego is an example of a company that has succeeded in achieving very high **effectiveness in variety**. This is because Lego pieces can be combined in so many different ways, to create different sets.

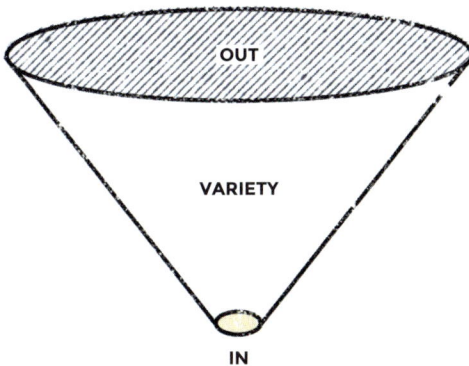

Let us take a look at what Lego actually does. How should you think in order to be like Lego? In other words, how can you be as effective as possible in terms of variety?

EFFECTIVE VARIETY

To begin with, we can say that different operations have different potential for offering variety. Many organizations and companies are similar to Hedberg's, and we have seen what they can do to compensate for their limited potential for offering effectiveness in variety. If we compare these operations with what Alexandra and Jenny do, we can see that these two women have created a different potential. What they do is to combine different things, either ingredients or items of clothing. They create variety by combining these different things in different ways with each other.

We call parts that can be combined with other parts **modules**. Both Alexandra Zazzi and Jenny Ragnwald use modules to cook nutritious and healthy meals or to create a wardrobe to improve your style. For Alexandra, modules are the base food items she uses in her cooking, and for Jenny, modules are the wardrobe basics. Combining different food items leads to the creation of different meals, and combining different items of clothing creates different outfits. This illustrates how Alexandra and Jenny are effective in providing variety.

VOLUME

High

Cost
efficienty

Low

MODULES

DISTINCTIVE
PRODUCTS

→ **VARIETY**

Low   High

Customization

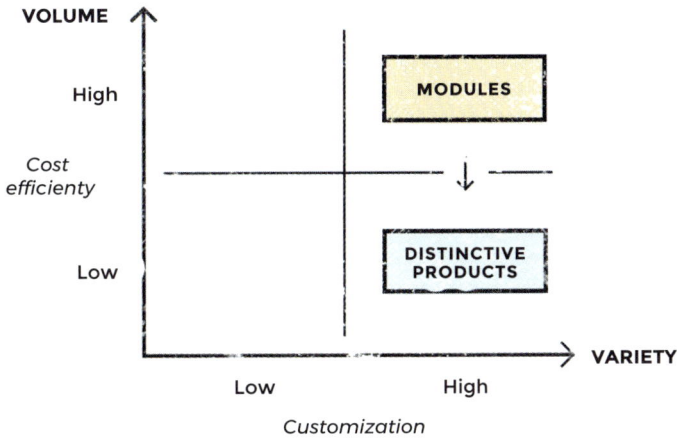

Turning again to Lego, we can see some other things that lie behind their success. First, what they offer is effectively infinite in the form of "creative and open-ended play." This product offer is communicated directly to the customer and expresses clear benefits and value that far outweigh what other toys can offer. Other toys can offer play, but few can offer the "creative and open-ended play" that Lego can. By doing so, Lego has created a very strong and clear competitive advantage.

Despite the fact that Lego uses few modules (Lego pieces), it can still provide a virtually limitless offer. The explanation is that Lego pieces are **variety-effective modules**, as they can be combined in an almost infinite number of ways. This is similar to what we saw earlier with Scania, where different parts can be combined to provide customized solutions. Therefore, to create **high effectiveness in variety**, which is the basis for offering a wide and ideally endless choice for customers, it is important that modules can be combined with as many other modules as possible. This will result in the ability to offer wide variety.

Lego and Scania have something else in common. They attach relatively little importance to the products, whether they are trucks or Lego sets. Instead, their focus is on what the modules can offer. Companies and organizations that concentrate their efforts on a single product run the risk of developing parts that can be used only in that one product and no other. This results in a low effectiveness in variety.

To Learn from Lego and **create high effectiveness in variety**, we can ascertain the following:

→ It is important to **formulate a clear product offer** that conveys directly to the customer what the real benefit and value is, such as "creative and open-ended play.".

→ It is important to identify the **units** that form the basis for variety. Units can be different depending on what is being provided and the type of industry.

→ Units that can be combined with other units are what we call **modules.**

→ When modules can be combined in many different ways, this leads to high effectiveness in variety.

SUMMARY
– CHAPTER –
FOUR

In this chapter, we have looked at what it takes to achieve effectiveness in variety.

→ Effectiveness in variety increases if what "goes in" can be combined in many different ways so that it leads to a wider variety in what "comes out."

→ Modules are the unit that forms the basis for high effectiveness in variety.

→ Modules will look different depending on the offers being provided and the branch involved.

→ To achieve high effectiveness in variety, it is important to provide the widest selection from as few modules as possible, which can be combined in a large number of ways.

In the next chapter, we will see how modules are also the basis for high efficiency in volume.

CHAPTER FIVE

VOLUME

Just as the last chapter explored effectiveness in variety, we will now take a closer look at the concept of volume and find out what we need to do to **be as efficient as possible in terms of volume**. We will build on earlier examples to see the role that modules can play in achieving high efficiency in terms of volume.

ONE METHOD AND THREE PRINCIPLES

To be effective in offering variety, and to guarantee effectiveness in terms of products offered to meet customer needs, we have learned that it is important to be able to combine modules in as many different ways as possible. Now, we will look at how to ensure high levels of efficiency within the modules that occur in high volume. This means that modules thus are the units that form the basis for achieving double competitiveness.

To help explain how to achieve this, let us return to **the method of modularization** and principles presented in chapter 3. The method describes an approach or way of thinking, and the principles act as guidelines for converting the products offered into modules. Let us look at the first principle, base modules.

Base modules

In the previous chapter, we met chef Alexandra Zazzi, who believes that cooking nutritious and healthy meals does not require a lot of extra time. To simplify the process, she divides all food items into five categories; produce, dairy products, conserved foods, dry goods, and frozen food. This provides a base structure for Alexandra when she is considering what nutritious and healthy meals to cook and also when planning what ingredients she needs to stock.

Stylist Jenny Ragnwald thinks along similar lines when helping a client to put together a wardrobe and develop his or
her style. Here, instead of base food items, she has wardrobe
basics, such as trousers, shirts, sweaters, jackets, and shoes.
These groupings help to give structure and guidance when
you are considering what you need in your closet.

Even Lego thinks along similar lines. In Duplo, for the
younger children, there are four blocks that recur in most of
the different sets. These have the same base function as the
base food items or the wardrobe basics, and they create order
in what is available. **Base modules** are simply the modules
that divide what is on offer into suitable categories.

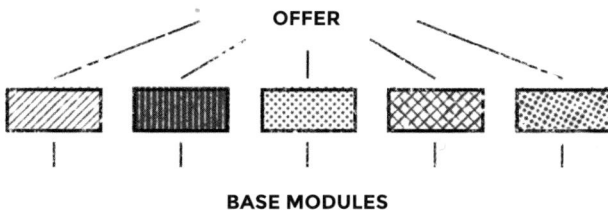

Variation modules

Now that we have defined a base module, the next step is to
decide exactly which variations each base module needs. We
call these **variation modules**. In relation to cooking, variation modules are the food items we need to include in each
respective base module. If we consider the base module of
produce, then onions, carrots, broccoli, and avocados could

be examples of variation modules. In our closet, we have base modules such as pants, to which we could add variation modules of jeans, cargo pants, wool pants, and so on.

Variation modules have a very important function as they must allow for a menu to be sufficiently varied, or to help us decide which item of clothing we need to add to our wardrobe to provide us with a suitably wide selection of outfits. Variation modules allow for variety and the ability to customize, which provides lots of different choices. Lego pieces in only one color or size would not lend themselves to the same kind of creative and open-ended play, for instance. Variation modules therefore make it possible to create the variety necessary to meet different customer needs.

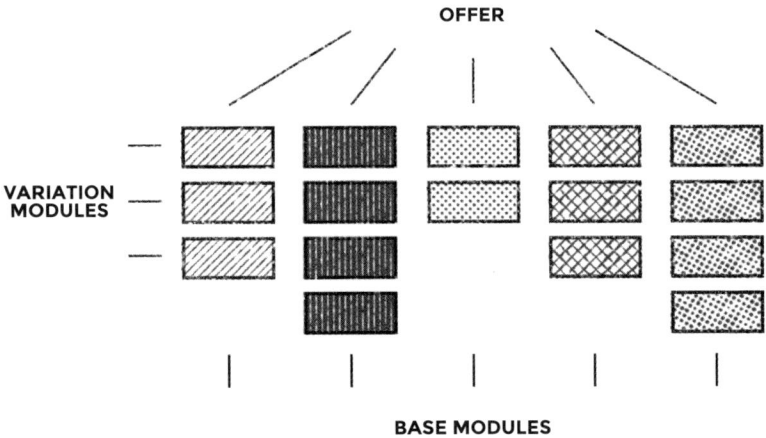

OFFER

VARIATION
MODULES

BASE MODULES

Although variation modules can create variety in the products offered, they also mean an increase in the total number of modules. This means that the number of variation modules cannot be too many. Otherwise we would end up with an overly full refrigerator, we could not afford to buy all the food, and our shopping list would be so long that it would take us ages to find all the items in the store. Therefore, we do not want either too many or too few variation modules. We need just the right amount, and this requires careful analysis of exactly what your customers need.

Interfaces

Once base modules and variation modules have been identified, they can be easily presented in a matrix, which will clearly show the modules that are required and included in the products on offer. To achieve high effectiveness in terms of variety, as we have noted, it is important for modules to be combined with each other in as many different ways as possible. This is possible with the help of the third principle, **interfaces**.

Interfaces differ depending on the type of products offered. For Lego, the interfaces are the studs on the top of the brick, which provide the ability to connect it to the underside of another brick, as well as the size and thickness of the pieces. If Lego pieces did not have these interfaces, that would certainly affect the creative and open-ended play for which the company is distinguished. Without these interfaces, the pieces would be non-functioning blocks that failed to interlock. It is the interfaces that enable anyone to build something quickly and easily. These interfaces bring Lego to life, and appropriately the word Lego means "bring together" in Latin.

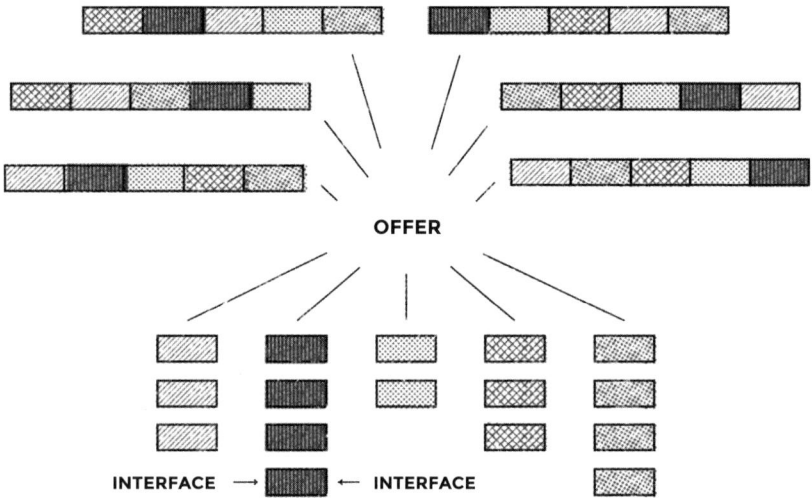

Interfaces will look different in different situations. For a chef, interfaces come in the form of recipes. Recipes contain information on how certain ingredients go together, how they can be combined, and in what quantities and how they should be cooked. For bus or rail services, transport time is a crucial interface that determines how different modes of transport can connect with each other, and it is reflected in the form of schedules. Schedules are essential for reliable transport systems and help to ensure the minimum waiting time for both road users and travelers alike. Interfaces have an important function in explaining how modules connect and can be combined with each other. The more modules that can be combined, the higher the effectiveness in variety.

HIGH VOLUME

We have seen how to achieve high effectiveness in variety through breaking down the products offered into two types of modules, which can be combined with each other through interfaces. We are now about to get to the heart of the book: **a high effectiveness in variety leads to high volumes in modules**.

Imagine that you have just bought a few different Lego sets from the store. When you get home, you tip them all out into one big pile on the floor. You then start to sort all the pieces into different piles such that all the pieces in each pile are the same. Quickly you will see that the piles of identical pieces start to get quite big. It appears that the sets, which are all quite different from each other, are largely composed of identical pieces. This is a tangible example of how modules enable wide variety in terms of the selection of different products available, but also enable high volume in parts.

The better an operation, like Lego, becomes at creating modules that are effective in offering variety, the greater the volume of parts produced. **Volume is hence a consequence of effective variety in modules.**

MODULARIZATION ELIMIMATES THE TRADE-OFF BETWEEN VOLUME AND VARIETY

Returning to Scania, in chapter 3 we learned that "The customer is at the center... the customer comes first," and that Scania's goal is to "customize solutions for each customer's unique requirements." We also discovered that modules create "a vast number of possible combinations with as few components as possible." It is clear that Scania not only puts the customer first, but also that it prioritizes variety first. The better Scania becomes at creating high effectiveness in variety, the greater the volume it can produce. The black swan from Södertälje devised **a method for generating high volume in common parts from high variety in distinctive product offers by using modules.**

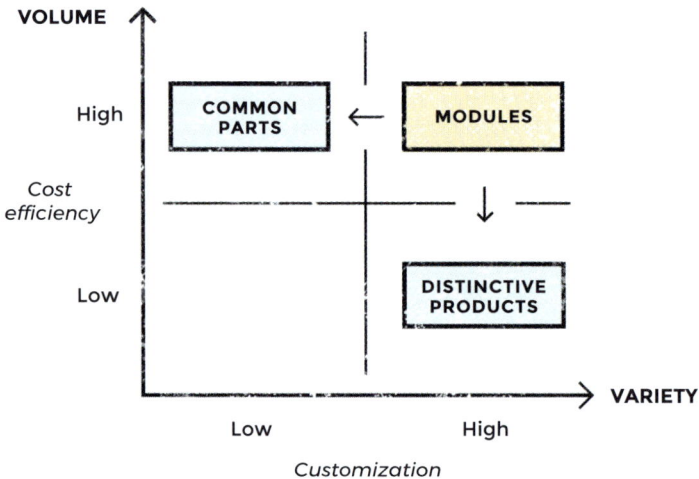

Taken out of context, this might sound strange. How can variety — which suggests diversity and differences — lead to high volumes? Surely volume should be low if variety is high, should it not? Intuition and logic suggest what we saw in chapter 2, that variety would be the natural opposite of volume. It is perhaps not surprising therefore that such reasoning is prevalent in textbooks and research articles, among people in general and among managers in particular. Many believe that variety must be low in order to achieve high volume.

A GUIDE FOR ACHIEVING DOUBLE COMPETITIVENESS THROUGH MODULARIZATION

Operations that achieve double competitiveness combine the advantages from both volume and variety. They utilize resources efficiently, as an operation can employ its personnel, knowledge, processes, machines, equipment, and materials in a way that adds values and is as efficient as possible. They create increased customer value by providing goods and services which are unique and tailored to each individual customer's needs in terms of features, functions, and performance levels, and which the customer really values.

Here is a **checklist** that summarizes the three steps necessary to implement modularization and achieve double competitiveness.

———————

STEP 1: Start by formulating **a clear product offer**, something that captures and articulates customer benefit and value. Think about Lego and its "creative and open-ended play."

STEP 2: Then divide the product offer into **two types of modules**:

↳ **base modules**, which provide the overall structure and categories for the product offer, and

↳ **variation modules**, which are necessary for creating increased variety in the product offer.

STEP 3: Finally, decide on the **interfaces**, which enable the modules to be connected and combined with each other.

———————

SUMMARY
— CHAPTER —
FIVE

In this chapter we have learned what it takes to be efficient in volume.

→ We have seen a method and three principles that form the foundation for structuring modules in such a way as to create:

    ↳ high effectiveness in variety, and

    ↳ the conditions for high volume.

→ We have seen that modules are the units that form the basis for double competitiveness, which means that high effectiveness in variety can be combined with high volume.

→ Operations that achieve double competitiveness succeed in high volume while also providing wide product variety.

In the next chapter, we will discover the benefits and values that this approach can provide for the climate and environment.

VALUE FOR THE ENVIRONMENT

We now know that modularization is a method that enables us to cope with both variety and volume. A combination that is otherwise difficult to achieve. Modularization provides us with other benefits too. In this chapter, we will look at how this method can **add value to the environment**.

VALUE FOR THE ENVIRONMENT

According to the World Wildlife Fund (WWF), our annual consumption of natural resources does not match what the world can produce; in fact, each year we consume about 50 percent more resources than nature is able to produce. We are thus depleting nature faster than it can regenerate. The Global Footprint Network each year estimates the so-called "Overshoot Day,"[1] or the day on which the annual production of the world's ecological resources is used up. In 1987, Overshoot Day was on December 19; in 2016, it fell on August 8.[2] In less than 30 years we have therefore dramatically damaged the situation for our planet.

Carina Borgström-Hansson of the WWF wrote the following in a press release:[3] "The cost of our mismanagement of natural resources becomes clearer day by day. Our ecological debt to future generations is in the form of deforestation, lack of fresh water, land degradation, loss of biodiversity and the build-up of carbon dioxide in the atmosphere which is the main reason the greenhouse effect grows stronger all the time."

Someone who took this situation seriously and has turned words into actions is Gunhild Stordalen. In an interview in Sweden's daily newspaper *Dagens Nyheter*, Stordalen explained how she became actively involved in getting the hotel chain Nordic Choice to run in a more sustainable way. She noted that the biggest environmental footprint left by the hotels' operations — nearly 70 percent — came from food and beverages. Three years ago she started asking which raw materials would be best for the climate, animals, public health, and the environment.[6] This led to the EAT Initiative, which Stordalen started in 2013 with a vision of reforming the global food system. Her efforts illustrate a way of thinking and acting within a specific industry sector to contribute to solving climate and environmental issues.

RESOURCE EFFICIENCY

Modularization is an environmentally friendly method; and that can be explained from two different angles, as we discussed in the previous chapter. The first angle involves using only a few modules to create an extensive set of product offers. Thinking in this way allows an operation to avoid developing modules that are not sufficiently used. This leads to using less resources and a more resource-efficient way of thinking and operating. The second angle is that the modules used are made in higher volumes, meaning that each module can be developed and designed in such a way that it can be produced in the most efficient way possible.

The following summarizes some of the advantages of modularization, considering it results in less waste throughout the entire value chain.

Development and design

Operations that work with modularization create advantages in development and design. An existing product or service does not need to be fundamentally changed to meet a new customer need. It is often sufficient to change the modules that are affected, or to develop a new module that complements or replaces the old one. This means that existing modules can be used again and again, even for new solutions. As a result, a company can respond quickly to new customer needs without having to invest heavily in development or design.

Purchasing

Because producing fewer modules leads to higher production volumes, advantages are also gained in relation to purchasing. More materials, knowledge, or parts of the same type can be purchased from the same supplier or partner, which often leads to lower purchasing costs. Higher volumes also lead to efficient administration, as the volume is not divided across several different involved parties. This in turn contributes to long and valued relationships where all are winners.

Quality

Having fewer modules establishes the foundation for better quality, as internal variation is less. An operation that works with modularization can concentrate its resources on the optimal design of each module, which means that it will be better tested and will result in the best design possible. This creates value for the customer, who receives a dependable and complete solution. It is also an environmentally preferable alternative, as in the long run it will lead to a more sustainable solution with less wasted resources.

Production

Having fewer modules is advantageous in the production stage as well. Industrial processes can be optimized to enable the most efficient production and assembly possible, and the same principle applies to service providers as well. Fewer modules also result in a lower overall consumption of resources the modules contain.

Administration and learning

Having fewer modules is essential for efficient administration. Work tasks can be broken down both within and between modules, which makes it easier to clarify roles and assign responsibilities, thereby creating significant time savings. There are resulting advantages in terms of learning, staff training, and teaching of work tasks. Having fewer modules simply means a lower internal variety while allowing for vast external variety.

Sales

Last but not least, this method has huge potential for improving sales. Customers can be segmented into categories and customer groups according to their needs, facilitating an understanding of what the product offer is and what the customer is attracted to. Even sales planning can be made more efficient with value being added to the process, and this is advantageous for training staff in the different products and services.

SUMMARY
—CHAPTER—
SIX

In this chapter, we have learned that modularization is a method which adds value for the environment. It is a built-in part of the concept.

→ It is the basis for a resource-efficient operation because:

    ↳ a few modules are sufficient to create a wide variety of available products, and

    ↳ modules are produced in high volume.

→ This leads to a lean value chain with resulting benefits in development, design, purchasing, quality, production, administration, sales and learning.

→ Modularization is the future for environmentally friendly methods that provide advantages for operations, customers, and society at large.

In the next chapter, we will look at how to create an operation that works with modularization to achieve double competitiveness.

CHAPTER SEVEN

DOUBLE COMPETI-TIVENESS IN SERVICE OPERATIONS

Let us now see how to **change and develop an operation** so that it can achieve double competitiveness. Let us take education as a starting point to see how modularization can be applied to knowledge-intensive operations and service industries.

EDUCATION FOR MANAGERS AND LEADERS

Executive education for managers and leaders is a big business, with turnover of close to one billion dollars annually in the US alone. Most colleges of rank have their own business school and offer executive education programs in addition to their undergraduate and graduate programs. The target group for these executive programs is managers and leaders who want to complement or refresh their existing knowledge and those who want to learn the latest and most up-to-date thinking within a specific subject area.

Profitability in this sector can be quite low, for various reasons. For your business school to be attractive and a relevant choice for people, it is important to offer a wide range of different programs, which is why these schools commonly offer everything from full-time MBAs which can take 1 year to complete, to part-time MBAs which can take up to 3 years. Longer executive education programs may include a total of 30 program days, spread out over a longer period of time; whilst programs within specific and niche subject areas may only be a few days in duration. Often courses are customized to suit specific customer needs, such as organizations in need of specific forms of help during a change process.

From my own years of experience in this sector, I know that executive education is a highly competitive market where quality is ultimately decided by participant satisfaction. The fees are high, and the already well-educated participants place heavy demands on the college in terms of the knowledge, quality, pedagogy, and overall experience they want to receive. The instructors are carefully hand-picked experts in their fields who have demonstrated teaching excellence. Both teachers and participants are evaluated regularly, often on a daily basis.

In my opinion, there are two reasons for low profitability in these programs. On one hand, it is important to offer **general** and comprehensive education courses in high volumes, where participants follow a predetermined schedule and course plan. One subject, such as finance or strategy, is taught one day, and on the next day a different subject is taught, and so on. On the other hand, it is necessary to offer **specific** programs tailored to match specific customer demands. This means that those who provide executive education need to work in two totally different ways, not dissimilar to the example of the subway and the taxi company that we examined earlier.

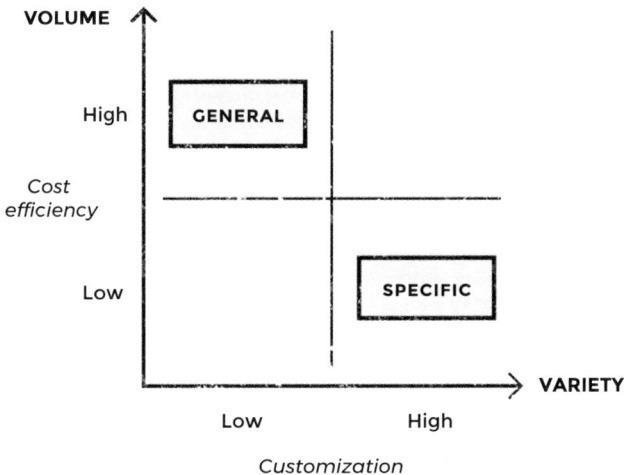

VOLUME

High   GENERAL

Cost efficiency

Low   SPECIFIC

VARIETY

Low   High

Customization

General and specific programs share few similarities, and this fact unfavourably impacts on profitability. The two types of programs place different demands on selling, marketing, and consultation, and since their content varies so greatly, they will have different needs in terms of development and design. Instructional staff will need to teach in different ways as the target group, structure, and content will differ. All this leads to higher costs and operations that lack internal synergies.

EXECUTIVE EDUCATION 2.0

Let us now help an operation in the executive education industry to achieve double competitiveness. We will do so by using the method and principles established in earlier chapters. The goal is to offer both general and specific programs and be profitable. To create Executive Education 2.0, we will apply what we have learned from earlier chapters and follow the three steps to implement modularization and achieve double competitiveness.

STEP 1: Start by formulating a **clear product offer** that encompasses and articulates customer benefit and value. Think about Lego and its offer of "creative and open-ended play."

STEP 2: Divide the products offered into **two types of modules:**

↳ **base modules,** which provide the overall structure and categories within the offer, and

↳ **variation modules,** which are necessary to create the increased variety within the offer.

STEP 3: Finally, decide upon **interfaces** that make it possible to connect the modules to each other.

Step 1: Formulating the product offer

Lego is really a textbook example when it comes to formulating a product offer. Using "creative and open-ended play" as an example, try to find words or a concept that clearly explains customer value — something that is unique, positions you in the market, as the foundation for future competitive advantages.

When it comes to training managers and leaders, **knowledge** and **change** are two areas to consider including. They are appropriate for various reasons: knowledge is what the participants will acquire from covering all the different subject areas, and change is about putting this knowledge into practice. With the help of these words, knowledge and change, we can begin to encapsulate an offer. After this, we should find out the customers' needs for knowledge and change. This process involves in-depth analysis, interviews, studies, customer data, and observations. We need to do this if we want to fully understand different customer needs and keep our knowledge up to date.

NEED FOR KNOWLEDGE

EXPERT KNOWLEDGE	**LEADING CHANGE**
Experienced managers	Management team
SUBJECT KNOWLEDGE	**IMPLEMENTING CHANGE**
Junior managers	Employees

Expert

Nonexpert

NEED FOR CHANGE

Small — Large

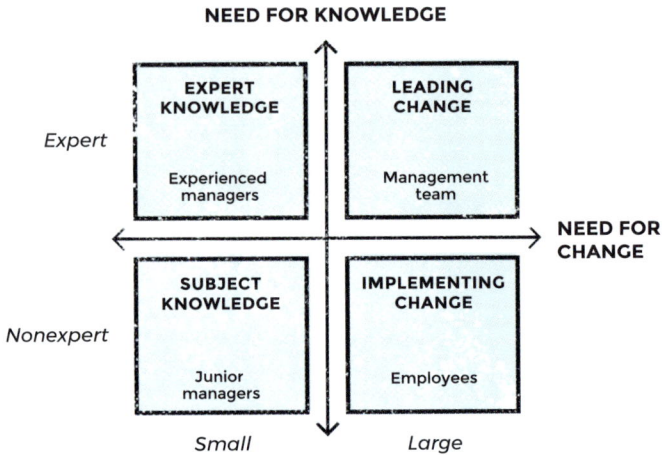

Data analysis shows that we have four different types of customer need emerging. Two are about knowledge, where the need is divided between experienced and junior managers. There are two different needs in relation to change: those who need models and tools to bring about change, and a more comprehensive need where a management team needs help to change an entire organization. This suggests a need for four different types of offers:

---

① **SUBJECT KNOWLEDGE:** for junior managers who want to learn more within all subject areas.

② **EXPERT KNOWLEDGE:** aimed at more experienced managers who have good knowledge within a certain subject area, but who seek to acquire current and advanced knowledge within that specific area.

③ **IMPLEMENTING CHANGE:** teaching participants about models and tools that they can use to bring about change.

④ **LEADING CHANGE:** about larger, strategic changes that involve the management team and will have great impact on the entire operation.

———————

Step 2: Identifying the modules

The foundation for the product offer is set. The next step is to identify the modules that should be included in the product offer. This can be compared to deciding the function of Lego pieces — e.g., deciding on the size, or whether they should be made of plastic or wood. As our example is about executive education, it is reasonable to assume that the modules will represent teaching and education, because this will satisfy the different needs within the framework for knowledge and change. We will begin by identifying the base modules.

Creating base modules

Base modules divide the product offer into smaller areas or parts. This can be likened to devising the categories that determine which different types of food, items of clothing, or Lego pieces we need. Through identifying base modules, which differ in terms of teaching methods or pedagogy, we also create opportunities for taking into account people's different learning styles and the fact that knowledge can be absorbed in different ways. This step also allows us to address the differences in experience and knowledge. That is why we need to create base modules that differ pedagogically. Here are a few examples:

LECTURES: a way of conveying and passing on knowledge in a subject area.

EXAMPLES AND STORIES: explain how theories and models can be put into practice.

CASE STUDY METHOD: working with a selected problem from the perspective of a particular model or theory.

INDIVIDUAL WORK: a way of finding real solutions, based on a model or theory, that will lead to creating real value in the participants' own operation.

DISCUSSIONS: opportunities for participants to share thoughts, knowledge, and experience.

These five base modules form the foundation for creating the product offer. But we also need to add some variety to these so that we can adapt programs to meet customer needs and be able to provide customized programs.

Deciding on variation modules

Let us think back to the strategies that Alexandra and Jenny employed when deciding on variation modules. Variation modules fulfilled a function by specifying the exact ingredients or items of clothing Alexandra and Jenny needed for cooking nutritious and healthy food or for effortlessly putting together a wide selection of outfits. Variation modules are therefore important for managing variety in a product offer. In our case, which is about executive education, we need to decide on the variations to offer within lectures, examples and stories, case studies, individual work, and discussions in order to meet the needs of different customers and customer groups.

LECTURES	EXAMPLES/ STORIES	CASES	INDIVIDUAL WORK	DISCUSSIONS
0 min	0 min	0 min	0 min	0 min
10 min	5 min	15 min	30 min	5 min
20 min	10 min	20 min	40 min	10 min
30 min		25 min	50 min	15 min
40 min			60 min	
60 min			90 min	

Through our analysis, we can see there is a need to create variation modules that differ in terms of time and content. An expert, for example, has the scope to assimilate more information in less time than someone with only a basic level of knowledge. Therefore, it is important to let the possible length of a lecture vary widely, it may not even be necessary to have a lecture, or 5 minutes may be sufficient, or it may require 60 minutes. In this way, a model or theory can be explained in different ways to different target groups.

The same logic can be applied in the other base modules. It is important that examples and stories can be varied in length and content to explain how a model can be applied in different situations. Similarly, different case studies can be used to explain a theory that participants are working on. If the program is about teaching participants to implement and manage change, it is important to set aside time for individual work. Therefore, we need variation modules that differ in terms of content and time allotted. Discussion can take place in both smaller or larger groups and can occur at the start, middle, or end of a theory session.

This step-by-step process shows how four different product offers that vary in terms of knowledge and change can be broken down into modules that meet different needs at both the individual and the management team level. Being able to combine these modules allows us to create thousands of unique programs — assuming that we have carried out the final step and designed interfaces that determine how modules can be connected and combined to create customized offers.

Step 3: Designing interfaces

Because courses are held using different formats, on different dates, and at different times for different participants, *time* is a very important interface. Time has already been built into our variation modules because they vary in length. However, we need to design an interface to connect these modules. Connecting different modules is necessary so that one can illustrate a theory or a model with suitable examples or stories, or describe how a theory or model works in practice. We need to be able to connect a model or theory with individual work, a case study, or a discussion. In these instances, interfaces involve how to connect modules to provide as much variety as possible. This allows for customized solutions that satisfy the demands of different target groups with very different needs.

VALUE FOR CUSTOMER AND SELLER

The model we used earlier to identify and formulate our product offer is an excellent starting point for selling our products and engaging with customers. It establishes a good foundation from which to understand the customers' needs for knowledge and change, and to explain the differences in format, pedagogy, and customer value that the four different product offers aim to deliver. The customer can be an active part of the process by understanding the differences, influencing how the product is assembled, and watching as it is customized to suit that customer's specific and unique needs. This process helps you to meet customer needs and expectations, whether you are meeting with an individual participant or with an entire management team.

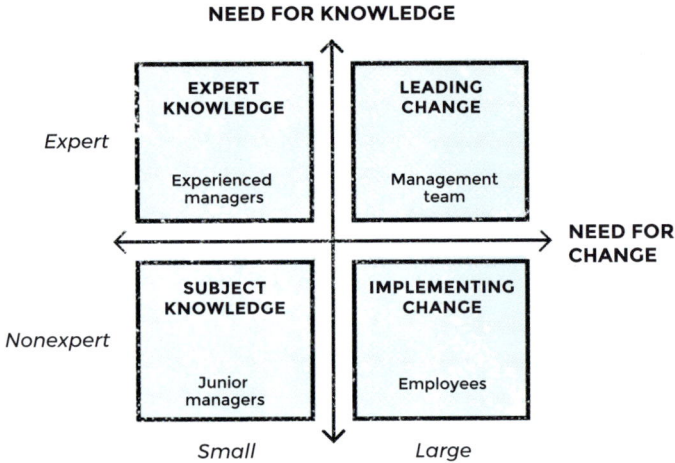

NEED FOR KNOWLEDGE

EXPERT KNOWLEDGE	**LEADING CHANGE**
Experienced managers	Management team
SUBJECT KNOWLEDGE	**IMPLEMENTING CHANGE**
Junior managers	Employees

Expert

Nonexpert

NEED FOR CHANGE

Small   Large

The model also provides advantages in marketing and brand building. It makes it easier to talk about an operation, what it has to offer, and how that offer differentiates itself within the market. The brand becomes clearer and unified. In this way, you can communicate more clearly with customers and other stakeholders and more persuasively present your unique product offer in comparison to those of your competitors. Employees also find it easier to form a shared picture about what the operation actually does.

When the structure and the modules are in place, it is easy to find the right teachers who are knowledgeable in their subject areas and who can understand the

importance of being able to adapt and tailor their pedagogical styles. Modules can also help faculty to develop
new examples, exercises, and case studies. Moreover, they
create clear links between all the various subjects taught
by different teachers.

Modules are a way of finding out what the market needs
and wants. By looking at what modules are popular, it is
possible to quickly assess performance and refine program
offers. Modules that are not so popular can be removed and
replaced by new ones, without impacting the other modules
or programs. Because the same module is used in different
courses, quality is also ensured, which in turn provides administrative staff with a clearer overviewThe model also
provides advantages in marketing and brand building. It
makes it easier to talk about an operation, what it has to
offer, and how that offer differentiates itself within the market. The brand becomes clearer and unified. In this way, you
can communicate more clearly with customers and other
stakeholders and more persuasively present your unique
product offer in comparison to those of your competitors.
Employees also find it easier to form a shared picture about
what the operation actually does.

When the structure and the modules are in place, it is
easy to find the right teachers who are knowledgeable in their
subject areas and who can understand the importance of being able to adapt and tailor their pedagogical styles. Modules
can also help faculty to develop new examples, exercises, and

case studies. Moreover, they create clear links between all the various subjects taught by different teachers.

Modules are a way of finding out what the market needs and wants. By looking at what modules are popular, it is possible to quickly assess performance and refine program offers. Modules that are not so popular can be removed and replaced by new ones, without impacting the other modules or programs. Because the same module is used in different courses, quality is also ensured, which in turn provides administrative staff with a clearer overview.

SUMMARY
– CHAPTER –
SEVEN

In this chapter, we have shown how you need to think to create double competitiveness in an operation.

→ We have used our three-step guide that describes how to achieve double competitiveness from modularization:

    ① Formulate a product offer.

    ② Identify modules:

        ↳ base modules

        ↳ variation modules.

    ③ Decide on interfaces.

→ We have seen how value is created for customers and sellers in the form of:

    ↳ tailored and customized product offers

    ↳ advantages for the operation through resource efficiency.

In the next chapter, we will discuss what to consider in relation to strategy and business development to achieve double competitiveness.

STRATEGY AND BUSINESS DEVELOPMENT

In this chapter we will focus on strategies and business development. We will see how easy it is to develop and change operations with **double competitiveness**, but we will also learn about the pitfalls and risks we need to be aware of to keep us on track.

STRATEGIES AND BUSINESS DEVELOPMENT

Let us look once again at the model that explains the logic behind achieving double competitiveness. The modules in the top right-hand corner of the figure represent the basis for an entire product offer. If these modules are combined in different ways, we can offer many different products. This is the foundation for effective variety, which in turn leads to high volume.

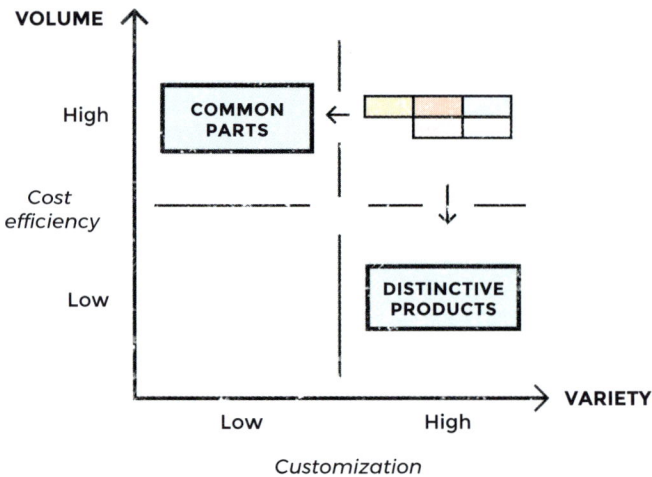

Using the model as a starting point, we will look more closely at issues surrounding **strategy and business development**. We will begin by looking at the example of a business that has gone through different growth phases and see how it has been affected.

ESTABLISHMENT, DEVELOPMENT AND GROWTH

In 2009, the Jonsson brothers started a cleaning company. They observed an increased demand for cleaning services, especially for monthly cleaning at a fixed price. Things went well for the company right from the start. During the first year, sales reached $380,000 dollars and the operating margin was 7%. Motivated by this early success, the Jonssons decided to try to double their profits. Their main strategy was to convince customers to buy cleaning services twice a month instead of monthly. Their efforts paid off, and in 2010 their sales reached $800,000.

The brothers carefully analyzed their market and believed that there were plenty of potential customers in their local neighborhood. They approached these potential customers, and many indeed took up their cleaning offer. Their operation grew by 43% and they managed to maintain their 7% operating margin.

By 2012, the market for cleaning services was flourishing, many new businesses were emerging, and the competition began to affect the brothers' business. They believed that expanding geographically would not prove profitable as it would mean increased travel time for their staff, which customers would not be willing to pay for. They therefore decided instead to expand the services they offered, such as "deep-cleaning" services and total house cleaning in conjunction with a move. The staff required training to carry out these new services, and new equipment had to be purchased to do the more thorough cleanings that the company now offered. Customers were pleased with these new services, and the deep-cleaning service was particularly popular for people who wanted their houses extra-clean for special occasions. Even the moving-related house cleaning services proved successful, and soon the company had achieved a turnover of $1.7 million. The new services had resulted in high costs, and therefore the operating margin dropped to 4.8%, but the brothers still considered the expansion worth the investment.

One day, the younger brother suggested expanding further by offering their services to companies as well as private households. The older brother was skeptical, however, and came up with many arguments against the idea. For example, he pointed out that offering cleaning to companies would involve moving into a different market, requiring new, specialized equipment and skills to cope with the large-scale cleaning involved. But the younger brother was very persuasive and had a counterargument for every objection raised, so in the end they began offering cleaning services to local companies.

Companies and households each had their own particular needs, and the staff found it difficult to differentiate between them. During talks with their accountant, the brothers realized that they had misjudged their investment this time. The new equipment was more expensive than they had anticipated, and the margins involved in cleaning for companies were lower than expected. They also found it difficult to

STRATEGY AND BUSINESS DEVELOPMENT

schedule their employees' time. Some employees had very long work days while others thought that they had too few work hours. The brothers had made an error in judgement. Sales decreased, they experienced negative operating margins, and employees began to resign.

Strategies for growth

The company went through different phases in their development. Three phases proved successful, but the fourth phase did not. Why did things go so badly off track for the brothers? How can we gain an understanding of what went wrong? Mathematician and researcher Igor Ansoff developed a matrix, defining four possible alternatives for growth, which can help our understanding here. He believed that growth can happen in only two dimensions: through change in products offered or through change in the market. Changes along these two dimensions leads to four possible growth strategies:

---

① Growth through **MARKET PENETRATION**. This is about selling more of an existing product within an existing market by beating or eliminating the competition.

② Growth through **MARKET DEVELOPMENT**. This is about selling more of an existing product to new customers in new markets, new places, or new countries, perhaps requiring new packaging and/or working through new channels and segments.

③ Growth through **PRODUCT DEVELOPMENT**. This is about introducing new products to existing customers within an existing market.

④ Growth through **DIVERSIFICATION**. This is about introducing new products to new customers in new markets.

Using Ansoff's four growth strategies, we can see how the brothers' business developed and changed over time. The first growth strategy, **market penetration**, is about selling more of an existing product to existing customers. The brothers undertook this strategy when they encouraged their customers to buy cleaning twice a month rather than once a month. This involved no change in the product offer or the customers, or in relation to the modules. It is therefore a cheap and and safe strategy. It is also an effective strategy, as it is aimed at customers with whom the operation already has an established relationship. Simply put it is about selling more of what they had to existing customers.

After this, the brothers changed their strategy and moved into **market development,** trying to find new customers in a wider geographical area. The products offered were the same, so again the modules were not affected. They sold more of what they already had, but now they reached out to more customers. Even this was an effective strategy, as it was relatively inexpensive and involved little risk because the products offered were unchanged and did not need to be adapted. New customers were reached through marketing and direct approaches.

Following this success, the brothers made big changes. They expanded the products offered through **product development**, adding two new services. This third growth strategy involved adding new modules to the existing module structure so that they could offer the new services. This is illustrated in the figure below, in which two new modules are added to the existing modules. This is a cost-efficient growth strategy, as to a large extent it is still based on previously existing modules.

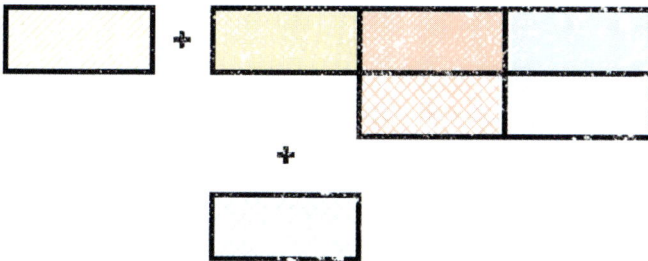

When the brothers adopted the fourth growth strategy, **diversification**, they experienced problems. They failed to appreciate how this strategy involved an entirely new structure, with new modules required to offer the new services to the companies. The difference was so great that they essentially needed to be a new company, since they were moving into an entirely new business area. The new activity needed to be organized independently from their other operations, as the modules were so different. It was an expensive lesson. Profitability and operating margins suffered. Diversification generally has a dramatic effect on modules and their structure.

By looking at the four growth strategies in combination with modules, we can create a powerful foundation from which to analyze issues that are otherwise difficult to grasp. The first two strategies affect neither the offer nor the modules. They are risk-free in that regard and also low in cost. Only when the offer is changed are the modules affected, which is logical. Product development has less impact on modules, as long as the new products are based on existing products and modules. Diversification, however, requires radical change and calls for an entirely new approach.

MERGERS AND ACQUISITIONS

Of the four growth strategies with which we are now familiar, **diversification** most resembles what happens in mergers and acquisitions. Even if two operations appear the same on paper, looking at them at the module level will reveal greater differences than initially perceived. This is because companies develop their modules in ways that are unique to each company. From a distance, it may look as if the "Lego pieces" are the same, but on closer examination, you see that they do not fit together. It is a bit like trying to connect wooden blocks with plastic ones.

Should operations that have achieved double competitiveness avoid mergers and acquisitions?

What we can take away from this analysis is that instead of running the risk of affecting modules in a way that subsequently turns out to be unproductive, it is better to transfer knowledge and experience so that an acquired operation can also learn about modularization. My advice is first and foremost to try to learn from experience, lessons, and principles.

STRATEGIC RISKS

Even if the benefits of modules are vast, you must be aware of strategic risks associated with them. For example, a standard can be changed so dramatically as to require fundamental changes in the module. One such example occurred when the old floppy computer disks were replaced by the USB memory stick. A similar thing is happening now with cloud-based solutions replacing the USB.

Another risk is that the value of existing modules could suddenly decrease due to shifts in knowledge. Suppose that, for some reason, it suddenly became outdated to eat "nutritious and healthy food." The value of that knowledge and those modules would fall. Changes in regulations have the same effect. In China, electric cars are rapidly replacing conventional cars, and electric cars are manufactured in different ways, with different modules.

```
         ┌─────────────────────────┐
         │        SUMMARY          │
         │     -CHAPTER-           │
         │      EIGHT              │
         └─────────────────────────┘
```

In this chapter, we have seen how modules also represent an important framework for understanding strategy and business development.

→ Modules are affected in different ways depending on which growth strategy is applied:

    ↳ where only the market is changed, the modules are not affected

    ↳ modules are more radically changed by product development and diversification, when operations enter new markets with new product offers.

→ Mergers and acquisitions can have a major impact on modules, and interfaces may need to be fundamentally changed.

→ Modules are inert and hard to change, which can lead to strategic risks.

In the next chapter, we will take a closer look at leadership and management in operations that achieve double competitiveness.

LEADERSHIP AND MANAGEMENT

How can you **lead and manage operations** that have achieved double competitiveness through modularization? What issues will be important for the board of directors? What should a managing director and their management team be thinking about and doing? What tasks and responsibilities should middle managers undertake? These are some of the questions we will consider in this chapter.

LEADERSHIP AND MANAGEMENT

The model for strategy and business development that we used in the previous chapter, shown again below, will help to explain the responsibilities and tasks involved in leading and managing operations that achieve double competitiveness. Using this model as a guide, we will take a closer look at the issues that the board, managing directors, managing team, and middle managers should take into account when leading and managing their operations.

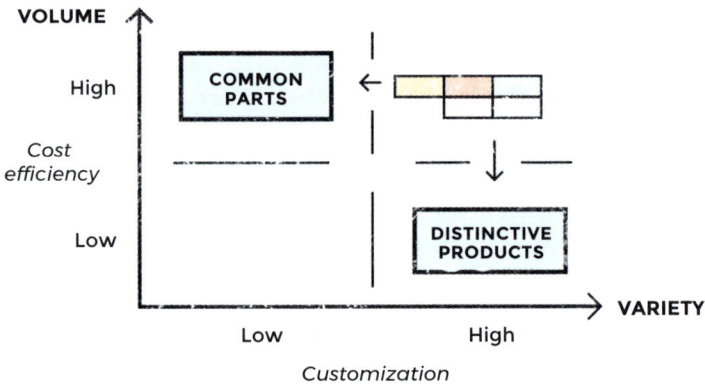

The board

The board has one task that is more important than any other. That task is to appreciate that the foundation for the company's competitiveness lies in its modules, as these allow for high effectiveness in variety. It was mentioned earlier that very few Lego pieces are required to achieve an unlimited product offer while at the same time establishing the conditions for high production volumes. This is fundamental to achieving double competitiveness, and it must be preserved at all costs. It forms the basis for competitive advantage and high revenues, and it creates a very advantageous position for sustaining such operations.

The board and management must also understand that modules define the boundaries for the products and services offered. However, neither Lego nor Scania is particularly limited in what they can offer, as their modules can be combined in so many different ways. On the other hand, neither Lego nor Scania offers sets or trucks containing modules that do not already exist. Modules therefore define limitations for how operations can grow, which is especially important to consider in acquisitions and mergers where modules will be shared between companies. The board therefore needs to ensure that it creates a new business area, rather than aiming to fully integrate both companies. Otherwise, the combination will threaten the operation's ability to be both efficient and effective.

It is very important for the managing director to fully grasp that the key to high volume comes from effective variety, and not vice versa. As this aspect of understanding and knowledge is so fundamental, it is crucial for the board to ensure that everyone, and not just a few individuals, knows this. This understanding must be shared across the entire operation and integrated into all processes and procedures. Even strategic documents, business plans, and financial reports should be built around the module structure.

RESPONSIBILITIES AND TASKS FOR THE BOARD

● The most important task facing the board is to understand that high effectiveness in variety leads to double competitiveness. This means that the knowledge about the company's equivalent of the **"Lego pieces that can be combined with each other"** is the basis for both different sets and high-volume production of pieces.

● Another important task is to ensure that modules are **not mixed together** in uncontrolled ways between operations, especially following an acquisition or merger. If the interfaces do not work together, there is a risk the operation will fail to benefit from both competitive advantages.

● A third task is to make knowledge about effective variety and modules **part of the structure**, of the operation — its processes, procedures, and documents. This knowledge will then be built into the organizational structure and disseminated among employees, increasing the company's value.

The managing director and the management team

The managing director's most important task is to make sure that modules are developed and maintained in the best way possible to ensure a viable and functioning entity. The managing director must ensure that the whole management team is fully aware of all the different modules, so that people will not be influenced by initiatives that could damage how the modules function or how they can be combined. During periods of great change, such as when the market or the product offer is altered, the general rule is to organize initiatives under separate business areas. Smaller initiatives, however, can often take place within the existing organization.

It is important for the managing director to work with a management team who understand that double competitiveness is achieved through the operations ability to create high effectiveness in variety. They need to understand that this capacity arises from an in-depth understanding of customer needs, and then they must be able to translate these needs into qualities and attributes that add value. Primarily, this is the work of the marketing and sales teams, but as the products' characteristics need to be translated into modules, this process is also linked to development, purchasing and production. Lego's success is based on the fact that each piece is a carrier of "creative and open-ended play" which becomes activated when connected to another Lego piece. The top priority is to ensure effective variety.

The management team has a shared responsibility to ensure that everyone in the operation understands the connection between what is being offered and the modules — that is, how "creative and open-ended play" relates to the "Lego pieces." This understanding is the link between strategic and operational decisions, and it allows for a more transparent and visible organization that can act from a shared and common understanding. Operations that achieve double competitiveness can be strategically quicker in their thinking and faster on their feet if everyone in the organization understands the connection between the products offered and the modules. This provides valuable advantages about which operations that are either effective or efficient — but not both — can only dream.

RESPONSIBILITIES AND TASKS FOR THE MANAGING DIRECTOR AND MANAGEMENT TEAM

● The most important task for the managing director is to ensure that modules are developed and managed in a way that is **reliable and takes a long-term approach.**

● The management team's most important task is to ensure that members of the operation understand the advantages of being efficient and effective, which is the **overall ability** to create high effectiveness in variety.

● The management team is responsible for ensuring that the entire organization understands the connection between the products offered and the modules. This creates the conditions for providing an **equally strong product offer** to Lego with its "creative and open-ended play."

Middle managers

Middle managers carry the operational responsibility for developing and changing modules in the right way. Here there is an important difference between base modules and variation modules. As we know, base modules describe a structure for how a product offer can be divided into different sections — for example, Lego pieces into different colors or sizes, or types of clothing in your closet. This categorization rarely changes. Lego has used the same categorization since the 1950s; the structure for clothes in a closet may change only every ten years. Other sectors may change more frequently.

Irrespective of the sector and the frequency with which base modules change, there is always a much quicker rate of change in the variation modules. This is where middle management is responsible. Characteristics, functions, and attributes must be implemented quickly so that each variation module has the greatest possible competitive advantage. Therefore, it is important to regularly evaluate the variation modules and find out how well they are selling, the volumes being sold, to which customers, and how profitable they are. Modules that do not sell well should be removed, to leave room for new ones and to free up resources.

It is important to fully understand customer needs. Design and development need to interpret and translate these into modules. Those who work within production, whether the product is a tangible item or a service, need to work with

Lean production and produce the highest volume possible. Purchasing can then optimize this high volume and minimize expensive variety, so as to achieve the best purchase prices possible. In this way, work can be coordinated within and across modules. The assignment of task, roles, and responsibilities can be simplified if an operation's structure is built around its module structure. Bigger issues are dealt with by the person responsible for the module concerned, and then handled within each module. This allows for efficient work processes and excellent use of resources.

RESPONSIBILITIES AND TASK FOR MIDDLE MANAGERS

● Middle managers have operational responsibility for developing base modules and variation modules. Most change occurs in **variation modules,** because this is where new attributes must be introduced to ensure competitive advantage.

● Another important task is to continuously **evaluate variation modules** to find out which ones are selling, how much they sell, and to which customers. Those that attain low volume should be removed to avoid unnecessary use of time and resources.

● A third task is to **lead and manage work at the module level.** This is advantageous in coordination and administration, so as to allow for an efficient use of resources.

SUMMARY
–CHAPTER–
NINE

In this chapter, we have looked at issues relating to the leadership and management of operations that have achieved double competitiveness through modularization.

→ The board needs to understand that high effectiveness in terms of variety must be controlled and managed, as this is the foundation for combining the two competitive advantages.

→ The managing director needs to ensure that modules are developed and managed in ways that are reliable and take a long-term approach.

→ The management team needs to ensure that operations understand the advantages of achieving double competitiveness, and that this arises from having a high effectiveness in terms of variety.

→ The central tasks for middle managers are to develop base modules and variation modules, recognizing that more frequent changes occur within variation modules.

The next chapter will take a closer look at finance and profitability for efficient and effective operations.

FINANCES AND PROFITABILITY

Operations that benefit from double competitiveness have a huge potential to flourish financially. This is because modularization can also lead to **double profitability** through the combination of high margins, high capital turnover, healthy cash flows, and cheaper operational financing. This chapter will take us through each of these gains so that we can see how together they result in a financially thriving operation.

FINANCES AND PROFITABILITY

The figure below summarizes the financial advantages that double competitiveness brings. We can see that a high level of customization results in high revenues, as the customer receives a product that has real customer value. We can also see that cost-efficiency leads to lower costs through high volume production which enable the efficient use of resources, processes, and activities. Combined, these can lead to double profitability.

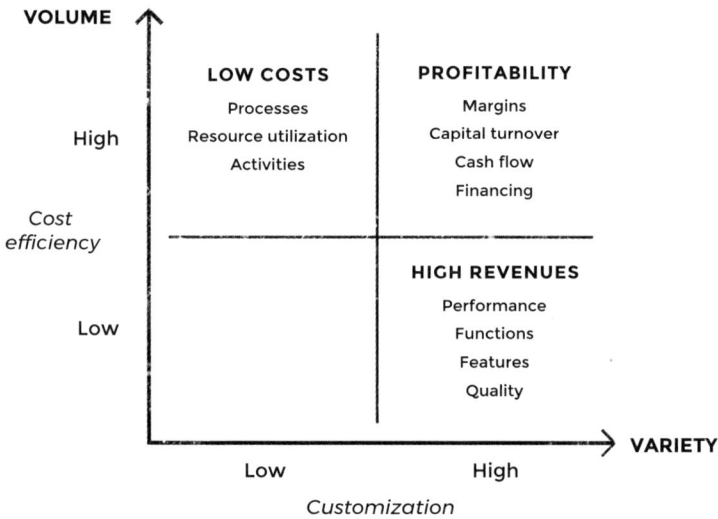

Let us now look at the top right-hand corner of the figure above and see how the separate points relate to each other. We will begin by seeing how we can create high margins.

Margins

Operations that have achieved double competitiveness can achieve high margins. This occurs through a combination highly customized goods or services — which means that customers are willing to pay for a product that provides real value — *together with* a high level of cost-efficiency, due to the efficient use of resources achieved through producing high volumes. It is through **combining high volumes with wide variety** that higher margins and double profitability are possible.

To achieve high revenues, one must deliver excellent customer value. Value increases if a good or service can be adapted or customized to match a customer's unique, individual needs. A customer who can see real benefits from a product, benefits that can be calculated in concrete financial terms, will be prepared to pay more for it. This means that if the product offers features that the customer has longed for, there will be a greater willingness to pay. Operations that can offer a high level of customization through variety can charge higher prices on the market than competitors that achieve lower levels of customization and offer less value.

High cost-efficiency is also essential to achieve **low costs**, and can be attained by producing modules in high volumes. This is because the utilization of machines, equipment, material, staff, knowledge, and information is high and resources are used efficiently. The result is reduced cost per unit produced, which is of course the basis for achieving cost advantages.

Operations that achieve double competitiveness optimize the trade-off between volume and variety, or cost-efficiency and customization, far more effectively than operations that only rely on a single competitive advantage. Operations that pursue only a single competitive advantage create margins from either high revenues *or* low costs, whereas operations that are both efficient and effective can combine the financial advantages of **high revenue** *and* **low costs** for optimal gain. This is what can double margins.

Capital turnover and cash flow

Another important advantage is that capital (knowledge, goods, assets) can be used over and over again. The impact can be seen in higher cash flows and cheaper financing. To demonstrate, let us look at the case of selling milk cartons.

For the milk at a grocery store to be fresh, the shelves must be restocked daily. New deliveries arrive in the morning and are sold by the end of the day. The same thing happens every day. This means that the stock of milk is replenished approximately 360 times per year. The store owner can use the revenues received by the end of the day to pay for the next day's milk delivery. This has several advantages over a lesser frequency of deliveries:

→ Because the milk is sold by the end of each day, the owner does not need to borrow money from the bank to pay for the next day's delivery. The owner can buy the milk with the money from the previous day's sales (cash flow).

→ The owner faces less risk of the milk becoming sour and having to be thrown out than if new deliveries took place less frequently.

→ The logistics are simpler, because fewer milk cartons have to be moved around the shop. It doesn't take much time to sort the cartons or many staff to carry out the tasks involved.

→ The owner does not need a huge store, which means lower rental costs.

The grocery store across the street does things differently. It buys twice the amount of milk, every other day. It sells the same amount of milk as its competitor, but it takes two days to exhaust the inventory. This means that the capital turnover is half that of the other store, the cash flow is slower, and the store requires twice as much storage space. Furthermore, it needs additional staff and requires more time to deal with the goods and the logistics.

The above examples show that a high capital turnover provides several important financial advantages. If we take the same reasoning and apply it to an operation that is both efficient and effective, the high capital turnover can be achieved at the module level. That is, the modules are sold and replaced in high volumes, not the products. This is because the modules are part of so many different products on offer. The completed goods or services that are comprised of modules are less interesting as a unit for analysis. **High capital turnover at the module level** is the important building block of high overall capital turnover.

Financing

Using the grocery store example, we demonstrated how several financial benefits are connected to each other. For example, a high capital turnover results in a faster cash flow, reduces the risk for obsolescence, leads to an effective value chain, simplifies work tasks, and reduces the need for larger premises. But there is still another advantage: the operation will be **cheaper to finance**, or cheaper to run. Let us compare the two grocers again — the one with daily capital turnover and the one that replaces stock every other day.

Assume that the first grocer carries grocery items with a total value of $3 million. Interest rates are 5%. This means that the grocer pays $150,000 per year in interest. The second grocer needs to carry twice as much stock, which means a total value of $6 million, and, assuming for the sake of this example that the interest rate is the same, they would pay $300,000 per year in interest. Therefore, the high capital turnover means that the first grocer spends only half as much to finance the store, a difference that leads directly to higher earnings. We can see in this way that operations achieving double competitiveness are cheaper to run than others. Operations tie up less capital, maintain a more favorable value chain, and have a less expensive balance sheet for their operations.

Profitability

With the help of the following figure, we can now summarize how margins and capital turnover work together to achieve higher profitability.

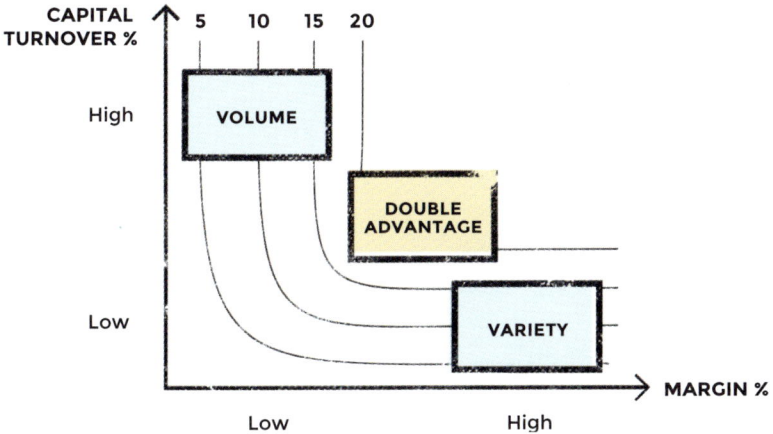

The dotted line shows different levels of profitability, and this will be the same no matter where on the the line you are. What we can see is that companies relying on only a single competitive advantage will find themselves on a lower profitability curve. Operations that have wide variety achieve high margins but low capital turnover. Operations that compete with high volume find themselves in the opposite position, with lower margins but high capital turnover. Operations that succeed in achieving double competitiveness through modularization can combine the financial advantages of both and therefore achieve higher profitability, through the interaction of margins and capital turnover.

SUMMARY
– CHAPTER –
TEN

In this chapter, we have seen how operations that achieve double competitiveness can double profitability.

→ This is possible through the interaction of several financial advantages:

    ↳ high margins

    ↳ high capital turnover

    ↳ strong cash flow

    ↳ less expensive financing.

→ Profitability should be managed, measured and controlled at the module level rather than at the product or product offer level.

EPILOGUE

You should now have a sound understanding of **what you can do** to create and develop operations that achieve double competitiveness from modularization and can thereby benefit from two types of value that are otherwise difficult to combine. In this epilogue, we will finish by summarizing what we have learned.

MODULARIZE TODAY TO BENEFIT FROM COMPETITIVENESS TOMORROW

At the start of this book, I stated that my own long-held view of competitiveness had been somewhat narrow and simplistic. For many years, I had equated creating value with having one clear competitive advantage. What led me to write this book was the insight that it is possible to combine two advantages and thus achieve double competitiveness, as Scania has done through combining the advantages of volume with variety. I came to recognize modularization as **the method** that combines these two extremes.

The trade-off between volume and variety is evident in many different contexts. Rarely, if ever, do we see a decathlete or heptathlete beat an athlete who competes in only one event, such as the high jump or long jump. This is because concentrating our efforts is often rewarded. Benefit is gained from high volume — whether it is frequent repetition of the same event in track and field or constant production of the same item in a factory. In both cases, the focus is on doing a lot of the same thing. However, our private and professional lives probably have more similarities to the decathlete or heptahlete than to the athlete who competes in a single event. How many companies and organizations do just one thing? This insight has become clearer and clearer to me as I wrote this book. To be really good at something, we need to set boundaries and focus. At the same time, we know that most companies and organizations do lots of different things, just like the decathlete or heptathlete. There is a risk, however, of losing out by trying to do too many different things.

I am totally convinced that all companies and organizations, irrespective of what branch they are in, need to modularize if they are to survive in the long term. This is the smart choice; it is a resource-efficient method that benefits the environment, it creates value for our customers who receive customized solutions, and it is good for the company itself as it ensures profitability and increased competitiveness. You can clearly see this in the examples presented throughout this book: How Lego create a clear and strong product offer! What a chef or stylist do to create choice in menus or outfits without having to collect too great an abundance of food items or clothes! How Scania, one of the smaller companies in the world's toughest manufacturing sector, create customer value and achieve world-class profitability year after year!

When you see the value of modularization yourself, the next step is to transfer this way of thinking to the operations in which you work. It is easier than you think. It makes financial sense, creates customer value, and is necessary if we want to establish a sustainable global environment for our future. Modularization is a win-win-win solution for everyone.

Please feel free to contact me with any questions, reflections or thoughts. For my contact information, go to: martinskold.se.

Best of luck!

GLOSSARY

GLOSSARY

Various terms and concepts used in this book may be unfamiliar to some readers. I have attempted to **define and explain** them where they first appear in the book, but they are also listed here for reference.

165

Cost-efficiency provides advantages as low costs enable products and services to be put on the market at lower prices. Low costs are possible through an efficient use of resources; that is how well an operation can use and employ its people, knowledge, processes, machines, equipment and material.

Customization provides advantages in the form of goods and services which are tailored to meet each individual customer's requirements. This allows for higher price to be charged in the market because the customer is willing to pay for quality, features, functions and performance which create customer value and customer benefits.

Single advantage from single competitiveness is when an organization, at best, is relying on only one out of two possible competitive advantages. They are either aiming for cost-efficiency or customization.

Double advantage from double competitiveness is when an organization combine the competitive advantages of cost-efficiency and customization and create a smart, profitable and coherent whole.

A module is a part of a product that can be combined with another part (or module) to provide and create variety in the products offered along with high volumes in the production of the modules.

Base modules divide the products offered into parts that are necessary to provide the products offered. Examples could be ingredients for a meal, items of clothing, or Lego pieces.

Variation modules create variety in a set of products, such as foods, items of clothing, or Lego pieces. They are important for meeting different customer demands.

Interfaces describe how modules can be connected or combined with each other.

NOTES AND REFERENCES

Following is **a summary**, chapter by chapter, of the references used in this book: scientific research articles, books, webpages, and newspaper articles.

CHAPTER ONE

Chapter one describes how **the potential for double competitiveness** can be realized when an operation combines cost-efficiency in the best way possible with goods or services that incorporate greater customer value from customization. The challenge is to combine both, as each has a different logic and way of working behind it.

① Drucker, P. 1977. *People and Performance: The Best of Peter Drucker on Management,* New York: Harper's College Press, 1977.

② Porter, M. E. 1980. *Competitive Strategy: Techniques for Analyzing Industries and Competitors*, The Free Press, New York.

CHAPTER TWO

Chapter two considers **why it is difficult to achieve double competitiveness** and why most operations tend to display only one advantage. Several explanations for this pattern have been presented in different areas of research.

One explanation (Slack et al.) as to why operations differ is that volume and variation require different resources and activities. Another (Porter) states that volume and variation have their basis in different competitive strategies: volume provides advantages through lower costs, whereas variation provides advantages from higher revenues. Another explanation is that volume provides economies of scale whereas variation provides economies of scope. This book contributes to knowledge by showing how scale (volume) and scope (variation) can be brought together into one theory, something that other studies have not done. A link for information on Stockholm's subway is also included below.

① Slack, N., Chambers, S. & Johnston, R. 2004. *Operations Management-* Prentice Hall, London.

② Slack, N. & Lewis, M. 2002. *Operations Strategy*, Prentice Hall, London.

③ Porter, M. E. 1980. *Competitive Strategy: Techniques for Analyzing Industries and Competitors*, The Free Press, New York.

④ Teece, D. J. 1980. "Economics of Scope and the Scope of the Enterprise", *Journal of Economic Behavior and Organization*, 1, 223-247.

⑤ Clark, J. A. 1988. *"Economies of Scale and Scope at Depository Financial Institutions: A review of the Literature"*, *Economic Review*, 73, 16-33.

⑥ Panzar, J. C. & Willig, R. D. 1981. "Economies of Scope", *American Economic Review*, 71, 268-272.

⑦ nyteknik.se/bygg/sa-langt-racker-1-miljard-6403890

⑧ sv.wikipedia.org/wiki/Stockholms_tunnelbana

CHAPTER THREE

Chapter three is **a case study on Scania** that has managed to release the potential that allows for double competitiveness from a method called modularization. Based on modularization, Scania can provide both customized products and achieve the advantages of producing high volume.

This chapter draws on various public documents such as financial reports and company presentations, as well as a large number of interviews with management carried out during 2013 and 2014. The following public references have been used in this chapter.

① scania.com/group/en/wp-content/uploads/sites/2/2015/09/Arsredovining-2014_tcm120-465262.pdf

② Tamme, T. 2009. *Från tumregler till ingenjörsvetenskap*, Tamme Publishing AB, Täby.

③ dn.se/nyheter/sverker-sjostrom

④ scania.com/group/en/wp-content/uploads/sites/2/2015/09/Arsredovining-2002_tcm10-16880_tcm120-54395.pdf

⑤ docplayer.se/10828663-Moduler-rapporten-modellen-for-framgang-sid-6-7-upp-fjarde-kvartalet-intervjun-vd-leif-ostling-om-2009-och-framtiden.html

⑥ nyteknik.se/digitalisering/darfor-friar-alla-till-scania-6453927

⑦ Sköld, M. & Karlsson, C. 2013. *Stratifying the Development of Product Platforms: Requirements for Resources, Organization, and Management Styles*, Journal of Product Innovation Management, 30, 62-76.

⑧ Sköld, M., & Karlsson, C. 2011. *Technology sharing in manufacturing business groups*. Journal of Product and Innovation Management, 29, 113-124.

⑨ Sköld, M., & Karlsson, C. 2007. *Multibranded platform development: A corporate strategy with multimanagerial challenges*. Journal of Product and Innovation Management, 24(6): 554–566.

⑩ Sköld, M., & Karlsson, C. 2012. *Product platform replacements: challenges to managers*. International Journal of Operations & Production Management, 32, 746-766.

CHAPTER FOUR AND FIVE

Chapters four and five describe what it takes to achieve **effectiveness in variety and efficiency in volume**. Chapter 4 explains the concept of variation and what is required to achieve *high effectiveness in variation*; Chapter 5 explores how to achieve *high efficiency in volume*.

To explain pedagogically how these can be combined, I have used chef Alexandra Zazzi, stylist Jenny Ragnwald, and the world's largest toy company, Lego, as examples. The information used in the examples is taken from the following sources:

① gp.se/matdryck/zazzismeny/1.579213--sakerna-du-bor-ha-i-skafferiet-#sthash.88XslVTj.OGHgnqs5.dpuf

② lyx.se/blog/2012/11/28/basgarderob-medpersonlig-stylist

③ dn.se/ekonomi/historik-over-legobygget

④ svd.se/kolossen-med-klossen

⑤ sv.wikipedia.org/wiki/Lego

⑥ dn.se/ekonomi/konsten-att-bygga-ett-imperium

CHAPTER SIX

Chapter six describes the **value and benefit** that can be gained from modularization. It discusses the resource efficiencies gained, creating a lean value chain, and the resulting reduction in operating costs. Using modularization is also an environmentally friendly strategy, a characteristic that is likely to become increasing important in the future. The following sources have been used.

① overshootday.org

② aktuellhallbarhet.se/jordens-resurser-forbrukas-allt-snabbare

③ wwf.se/press/aktuellt/1575826-nu-r-overshoot-day-hr-tidigare-n-ngonsin

④ stordalenfoundation.no

⑤ dn.se/ekonomi/global-utveckling/mat-mer-an-halsofraga-pa-toppmote-i-stockholm

⑥ dn.se/ekonomi/global-utveckling/stordalen-andrade-strategi-efter-bacon-gate

CHAPTER SEVEN

Chapter seven provides an example of how to change and **develop a service operation** so that it can achieve double competitiveness. The reason for choosing an example from

executive education is to show that the method and principles are equally applicable to operations centered primarily
on knowledge and services. Having worked extensively with
different operations within the field of executive education
for more than ten years, I have based this example on my
cumulative experiences and not on any specific operation.

CHAPTER EIGHT

Chapter eight explains important considerations of **strategy
and business development** for operations with double competitiveness. It looks at types of business growth and applies
a well-known model devised by Igor Ansoff, which is then
combined with the theory developed in this book. It then
discusses the reasoning surrounding mergers and acquisitions, along with the strategic risks involved.

① Ansoff, H. I. 1965. *Corporate Strategy: An Analytical Approach to Business Policy for Growth and Expansion*, New-York: McGraw-Hil.

② Leonard-Barton, D. 1992. "Core Capabilities and Core Rigidities: A Paradox in Managing New Product Development". *Strategic Management Journal*, 13, 111-125.

③ Henderson, R. M. & Clark, K. B. 1990. "Architectural Innovation: The Reconfiguration of Existing Product Technologies and the Failure of Established Firms." *Administrative Science Quarterly*, 35, 9-30.

④ Sköld, M. 2007. *Synergirealisering: Realisering av produktsynergier efter företagssammanslagningar, doktorsavhandling*, EFI, Stockholm.

CHAPTER NINE

Chapter nine is about **leadership and managing** operations that have achieved double competitiveness from

modularization. It looks at the necessary perspectives and responsibilities for the board, the managing director and management team, and middle management. No references were used in this chapter. I have based these comments on my own observations of how successful companies address these issues.

CHAPTER TEN

Chapter ten considers **finances and profitability**, explaining in practical ways how double competitiveness from modularization is more profitable. This is due to the combination of several financial advantages, such as high capital turnover, strong cash flow, and cheaper financing. Each aspect is explained along with their interaction. Operations with double competitiveness are more profitable because they combine two competing strategies and can achieve cost advantages and enhanced revenues. The following references have been used:

① Johansson, S.-E. & Runsten, M. 2005. *Company profitability, financing and growth: objectives, context and methods of management,* Studentlitteratur, Lund.

② Porter, M. E. 1985. *Competitive Advantage: Creating and Sustaining Superior Performance,* The Free Press, New York.

③ Porter, M. E. 1996. "What is Strategy?", *Harvard Business Review,* 74, 61-78.